Contents

talking
their way
into science

Hearing Children's
Questions and Theories,
Responding with Curricula

KAREN GALLAS

Teachers College, Columbia University
New York and London

for Nesta and Ed

Published by Teachers College Press, 1234 Amsterdam Avenue, New York, NY 10027

Library of Congress Cataloging-in-Publication Data

Gallas, Karen.
    Talking their way into science : hearing children's questions and theories, responding with curricula / Karen Gallas.
        p.   cm. — (Language and literacy series)
    Includes bibliographical references and index.
    ISBN 0-8077-3436-5 (alk. paper) — ISBN 0-8077-3435-7 (pbk. : alk. paper)
        1. Science—Miscellanea.   2. Science—Study and teaching (Elementary)   I. Title.   II. Series: Language and literacy series (New York, N.Y.)
    Q173.G32 1995
    372.3'5044—dc20   94-46906

ISBN 0–8077–3435–7 (paper)
ISBN 0–8077–3436–5 (cloth)

Printed on acid-free paper
Manufactured in the United States of America

02 01 00   8 7 6 5 4

LANGUAGE AND LITERACY SERIES

Dorothy S. Strickland and Celia Genishi, SERIES EDITORS

Acknowledgments

My research on Science Talks began in 1989 when I first joined the Brookline Teacher Research Seminar. At that time I started to tape and transcribe Science Talks, and with the help of seminar members began to try and make sense of them. In the early stages of this work, Sarah Michaels was extremely helpful to me, both because she encouraged me to pursue my interest and because she showed me how to look at complex data in a thoughtful and open way. Since then, the members of the seminar have continued to be interested and creative in their responses to the many transcripts I have shared. Their dedication to understanding children's intentions and meanings is always a source of support and inspiration.

Many teachers at the Lawrence School in Brookline, Massachusetts have also contributed in different ways to this book. Dianne Litts, Mary Sodano, and Ilene Miller opened their classrooms to me so that I could listen to Science Talks with their third and fifth grade classes, and they provided thoughtful observations about themselves and their children. Other teachers, in different ways, have raised important questions and provided new insights about their own and their students' use of the talks, including Susan Dempsey, Leslie Egan, Lori Geiger, Steward Golomb, Alicia Hsu, Ann Martin, Fran Strohm, and Ina Thompson. All these teachers have spent time talking with me about how Science Talks work, or don't work, in their classrooms. These discussions have helped me to think carefully about the evolution of the talks in my practice. I thank all of them for their generosity, curiosity, and dedication to their craft. Their spirit is also found in the pages of this book.

There are no shortcuts to be taken when whole class discussions are used as data. Entire talks must be transcribed, and the transcription process is onerous. Fortunately, at a few points in time I was able to secure small grants that funded the transcribing. I am grateful to the Massachusetts Field Center at the University of Massachusetts at Boston, and to the Literacies Institute, formerly at the Education Development Center in Newton, Massachusetts, for their support.

The writing of this book was made possible in part through my participation in an internship program with Lesley College Graduate School in Cambridge, Massachusetts. Through that program I was able to work with a wonderful intern, Cynthia Neff Gillespie, and also was released one day a week to work on this book. In addition, a grant from the Brookline Foundation, a nonprofit citizen group that supports staff development in the Brookline public schools, enabled me to participate in a summer writing retreat with Brookline Seminar members during which part of the work on this book was begun.

Special thanks go to Michael Rich, who volunteered his time and expertise as a pediatrician to work with my students. I learned a great deal from him about the human body and was delighted to witness what happens when a scientist and children *really* talk. Thanks also to Sarah Biondello and Brian Ellerbeck, of Teachers College Press, and most especially, Carol Collins, my astute editor.

Finally, although a great deal of this kind of research is obviously done in the classroom, when the day ends it all goes home. I am very thankful for the ways in which my family has contributed to my sometimes unbounded fascination with Science Talks. Both my son, Liam McNiff, and my daughter, Kelsey, have always humored me by talking about questions my students have asked. Kelsey, especially, has shown me that the wonder of childhood, if nurtured, can become a way of being in the world. Her questions and curiosity constantly contribute to my work with children. And of course I am indebted to my husband, Dave Edwards, who makes it impossible *not* to write.

talking
their way
into science

Hearing Children's
Questions and Theories,
Responding with Curricula

[The word] becomes "one's own" only when the speaker populates it with his own intention, his own accent, when he appropriates the word, adapting it to his own semantic and expressive intention. Prior to this moment of appropriation the word … exists in other people's mouths, in other people's contexts, serving other people's intentions: it is from there that one must take the word, and make it one's own. And not all words for just anyone submit equally easily to this appropriation, to this seizure and transformation into private property: many words stubbornly resist, others remain alien, sound foreign in the mouth of the one who appropriated them and who now speaks them; they cannot be assimilated into his context and fall out of it; it is as if they put themselves in quotation marks against the will of the speaker. Language is not a neutral medium that passes freely and easily into the private property of the speaker's intentions; it is populated—overpopulated—with the intentions of others. Expropriating it, forcing it to submit to one's own intentions and accents, is a difficult and complicated process.

—Mikhail Bakhtin, *The Dialogic Imagination,* pp. 293–294

Introduction

How do scientists know all that they know? Maybe they got
teached. Maybe they searched. Maybe they watched. Maybe they
thought about it.

—Donald, age 6

This book is about science. But it is also about a question. It is intended
to be a very focused look at one aspect of science teaching and learning: Talk. Within the realm of talk, it focuses on a very particular kind
of talk—that is, dialogue among children. It ponders, as Donald often
did, how one gains entry into a discipline, how one joins in on a conversation that is about life itself. It reflects the point at which wonder
moves hungrily into a search for knowledge.

Still, even as it is a very particular exploration of language, it spills
messily over into curriculum and methodology. Science Talks, as we
have come to call them, have taken a place as an integral part of my
science curriculum. They are distinguished from both the more formal
times when I "teach" science through direct instruction, as well as
those times when children work with science materials and activities.
Science Talks occur in a separate and formally prescribed time frame,
and within a whole class discussion format, and they are now recognized by both myself and the children as an integral part of our science studies.

What I will describe in this book is how our practice of Science
Talks developed in my primary classroom in response to my own
question as a teacher researcher. My reflections will focus alternatively
on what "real" science is, on the study of science in schools, on children as thinkers, on the role of theory in the science classroom, on the
nature of collaboration and discussion, on different kinds of talk, on
the acquisition of a discourse, on the teacher's role in science instruction, and on the social construction of learning. In this process I will
necessarily share the details of some of my work as a teacher researcher, and those details also will illuminate the ways in which the
act of teaching and learning evolved in my classroom.

IDENTIFYING THE QUESTION

When I began my work with Science Talks, I had a broad question: How do young children talk about science? At the time I wanted to explore the language children naturally used in science discussions *before* they had had much exposure to "school science," and I began to collect data in my first grade classroom using what we came to call "Science Talks" as a point of entry.

As a teacher researcher my research process always seems to embody the merger of my public, professional self, and my private, personal world in identifying questions to be considered. The questions I ask often identify those things that were absent for me as a child in school. Thus, as a formerly silent student, my research focused on the area that was most absent in the classrooms of my childhood: *talk*. And in asking this question, I wanted to understand the ways in which talk might open the world of science to children, a world that was closed to me as a child. As a teacher I had the intuitive understanding, which Bakhtin (1981) has more clearly and completely elaborated, that the essence of gaining competence in a field, of owning "the word," may rest in whether one can "appropriate" the language of that discipline, "populating it with his own intention, his own accent" (p. 294).

"Appropriate," in Bakhtin's context, is used as a verb implying a movement toward ownership of the word. It is a powerful verb that emerges from the determination of the individual to take control of a new way of thinking and being. I find it ironic that it is also a homonym for a word that can, in another social context, be its antonym, a word that was, unfortunately, much more active in my life as a student of science. I struggled to be "appropriate" in my science classrooms, that is, I labored to look, act, and talk in a way that my teachers would think was correct, or appropriate to the study of science, but in fact I never learned how to participate successfully in that world.

THE PROBLEM OF SCIENCE

I often point out in speaking about Science Talks to teachers and parents that I never talked about science as a child. In fact, no one I knew ever talked about science. It was a field that had nothing to do with my life; it employed a language in my native tongue that I could not speak fluently. As a result, I, along with many other children, came to the conclusion that I wasn't good at science. It seems sad that this notion of not being "good at science" lives on for many children today (and for their teachers), because after collecting data on science talk for 5 years I haven't yet met a child (or an adult) who was unable to think and talk like a scientist. I have met people who couldn't use the appropriate terminology or factual references about a scientific phenomenon, but they were all in full possession of a natural ability to question, wonder, and theorize about every aspect of the natural and physical world.

I believe that when a community of learners begins with the act of dialogue about the world, and when that dialogue occurs outside of the theoretical or conceptual influence of the teacher, it moves more naturally and vitally toward theory and a readiness for instruction and study. This is the point at which the appropriation of the discourse of science begins. In this process the students take on the voice *and the authority* of scientists. They begin to bring their world of experience to the classroom in the form of personal narratives and important questions, realizing as they do that what they observe, wonder, and imagine has importance in a science classroom. In this way teachers and children move purposefully together toward an inclusive kind of talk about science where everyone is admitted.

This is what Bakhtin might call a "heteroglossic" science talk: messy and sometimes chaotic in its style and content, but reflecting the vitality of children's lives and ideas; a "living" science language (Morson & Emerson, 1990) that is not prescripted or bounded by ideas about what might be appropriate subject matter or developmental expectations, but rather acknowledges that the desire to understand the most complex kinds of questions emerges in early childhood and should be nurtured at all costs! Achieving this goal requires time, a commitment to placing the child's voice in the foreground of the science curriculum, *and silence*—on the teacher's part. This book presents what I found out when I was finally able to accept and implement those requirements.

THE SETTING

Since 1989 I have audiotaped discussions with heterogeneously grouped classrooms where the science curriculum is taught by classroom teachers, and not by a specialist. I have collected data primarily from first and second grade children, but I also have participated in talks in third and fifth grade classrooms and have had numerous discussions with teachers from a variety of settings who have begun to work with this kind of science talk. Although the population of the school where my research took place is predominantly from professional families, the school is in an urban setting and the children represent mixed socioeconomic and racial backgrounds, with a moderate number of bilingual students.

While many of the talks cited in this book will focus on first and second grade children, I have observed that the dialogue that occurs within the context of Science Talks provides an important forum for children of all ages, and their teachers, to develop new ways to talk and think about science.

I do believe, however, that it is tremendously important to emphasize the contextualized nature of this piece of teacher research. In other words, what I have developed in my setting and the things I now understand about science talk are, on some level, localized. I am one teacher, with my own educational baggage, my own specific strengths, weaknesses, and interests, and I teach in a particular community with its own very particular population. As I describe this context, my particularities may or may not resonate with my reader.

What will resonate, I think, are the children's voices: the tremendous potential for complex thinking that they embody when spaces are made for them to act in concert, and the ways in which their voices make us long to go back and be prodded to think and imagine as children once again. Although those voices represent a specific population of children in this country, I would hope they urge other teachers and researchers to examine the discourse that develops in other settings with very different children and to further elaborate the many kinds of talk that a discipline might embody in the service of a more complete educational experience. This book, taken literally, is about *science* talk. Taken metaphorically, it is about acquiring a discourse.

NOTES ABOUT THE STRUCTURE OF THIS BOOK

Throughout the book, children's talk is included as part of the text, and transcripts of entire talks are recorded in Appendix B. In all these transcribed passages, the following conventions are observed:

T: refers to myself as the teacher.
T2:   is a second teacher or a student teacher.
Karen: is the name by which the children address me.
. . . :   represents a long pause.
[   ]:   indicates that the text that is bracketed is occurring simultaneously with the text just above it. In other words, more than one person is talking at the same time.

?:   Indicates that I could not identify who was speaking on the tape.

??: Indicates that a word or words were inaudible on the tape.

I have included full transcripts in Appendix B so that the reader can see two of the talks cited in their entirety. This will enable those interested in looking more closely at complete discussions to read through a full transcript. The reader should note that each transcript represents approximately 30 minutes of audiotaped discussion.

The sequence of chapters in the book is intended to move the reader from a general discussion of Science Talks to more specific topics that I have identified as particularly important. Chapter 1 reflects upon the nature of science, both as a way of approaching the world and as a form of discourse, and further examines the purpose of talk and discussion in the real world of science and in the microcosm of the classroom. It proposes that a hands-on, process approach to teaching science, while an important aspect of science study, is not enough.

Chapter 2 introduces Science Talks as a general classroom practice, discussing the most basic aspects of implementing the talks with a group of children. In Chapter 3, I "dismantle" the talks from a semantic point of view, to introduce the reader to the idea of looking closely at children's language both for how meaning is constructed and for the kinds of "talk behaviors" children exhibit in Science Talks.

Chapter 4 moves more deeply into a consideration of theory and how children build theories within the Science Talks. It explores the nature of theorizing and the kinds of intellectual and creative forces that are at work when children build theories collectively. The difficulties children have when they encounter a question that is too hard is introduced in Chapter 5. This chapter describes how children proceed when they are unable to build any coherent theory about a phenomenon and, further, how teachers can use Science Talks to uncover children's misconceptions and help them find ways to explore difficult questions.

The important role of misconceptions as a way to understand children's thinking is examined further in Chapter 6. This chapter describes the importance of soliciting children's "seminal" questions and thereby uncovering their deeply held theories about the world prior to a unit of study. In contrast, Chapter 7 looks at a question that was asked in the latter stages of a science unit and provided an opportunity for a group of children to move to more sophisticated and challenging levels of thinking.

Chapter 8 considers the role of Science Talks in building curriculum, describing a study of human biology that lasted over 12 months and was structured around children's questions. It emphasizes the importance of the teacher's role as observer and facilitator of children's interests. Chapter 9 adds another dimension to the teacher's role by introducing the process of coaching a class of children in how to talk together. It follows the development of a specific class of children as "talkers" and describes how the teacher acted as both model and coach in that process. Chapter 10 proposes that a more dialogic process of teaching and learning science, which attends closely to children's questions, theories, and prior knowledge, has the potential to change the field of science from an exclusive to an inclusive discipline.

CHAPTER 1

What Is Science?

The purpose of scientific enquiry is not to compile an inventory of factual information, nor to build up a totalitarian world picture of Natural Laws in which every event that is not compulsory is forbidden. We should think of it rather as a logically articulated structure of justifiable beliefs about nature. It begins as a story about a Possible World—a story which we invent and criticize and modify as we go along, so that it ends by being, as nearly as we can make it, a story about real life. (Medawar, 1982, pp. 110–111)

Considered from the standpoint of most teachers and students, we know that science is an intimidating and difficult subject. It presents a serious dilemma for all those who want to participate in it, and that is that as it evolves over years of schooling it often becomes a rigid, prescripted process where formula, rather than thinking, is valued. In schools science is represented as a particular kind of exclusive discourse that one must master, a dispassionate discourse that relies on special structures: on hypotheses, experimentation, the identification of variables, replication, logic, the understanding of paradigms, and above all an attitude of certainty. Most students of science never learn to use this discourse very well, and most teachers are intimidated by it. As a result, science is seen as a field for the talented few, and the achievement of real scientific literacy in this country is the exception, rather than the norm.

It is clear to me in thinking and reading about science that the way it is presented in most schools is a poor imitation of what practical science can be in the real world. What I experienced as a student, and what most teachers and students view as science, is an archaic model that emerged in the late nineteenth century (DeBoer, 1991). Despite periods of educational innovation in the twentieth century, this model has not grown to include the questions and the knowledge of the twentieth century: questions about the practice and authority of scientific knowledge and about the purpose of science education in a democratic society; new understandings of human development and the growth of intelligence, of the links between creativity and scientific achievement; and revisions in our views of what the "scientific method" really is (Duschl, 1990; Lemke, 1990; Medawar, 1982; Storey & Carter, 1992). What science teaching does reflect, however, is the separation that has gradually taken place between the world of the scientist and the reality of the lay public.

Certainly the language of science has become more narrowly defined and more exclusive. As I have pointed out, much of the teaching of science in my childhood was based on acquiring the "appropriate" language, on understanding the scientific method, on learning the proper procedures, on precision in measurement and reporting, and, as a result of these rigorous processes, on identifying who was scientific and who was not.

In reality, of course, science is not so neat and clean, and future scientists are not so handily identified. Like teaching and all dynamic and changeable professions, science is a creative and exploratory field that draws upon many kinds of knowledge. Yet in the process of translating a field of *practice* into the *study* of a field, the essence of the practice is lost, and the human resources that will fuel the development of the field are discouraged.

My classroom is filled with the "stuff" of natural and physical science. There are a variety of animals living in different habitats: a rabbit who hops around on a tether; salamanders, snails, slugs, and a variety of insects in a terrarium; a fresh water aquarium with fish, plants, snails, newts, and insect larvae; a pair of cockatiels that mate and raise babies in the spring; an exploratory table with rocks, shells, nests, and assorted other treasures from the natural world; changing centers on magnets, pulleys, the human body, dinosaurs, volcanoes, and so forth. These materials are the backbone of our science curriculum. They enrich it by providing ongoing experience with concepts such as habitats, animal families, and adaptation, to name a few, and they provide us with focal points for units of study, for example, on motion and speed. Further, they often stimulate the children to ask questions that we go on to discuss in Science Talks, and we return to them again and again as we search for answers to our questions.

I have provisioned my classroom this way because of my own strong interest in developing a rich science environment, an interest that has developed over time as I have begun to follow my instincts about those things that fascinate children. (I could say that I've begun to retrieve or discover my own fascinations, and that also would be accurate.) However, I was not a science major in college, and I do not have any special training in a particular field of science. Nor did I have much success as a student of science in high school and college. I have never had a course in the methods of teaching science, and when I examine why science is so central to my classroom I have to conclude that on some level I am filling in the gaps of my own education. In the process of teaching young children, I have rediscovered, through them, the joy and wonder that the natural world provokes. It is a response that celebrates the attitude of *not* knowing and wanting to find out; that requires that all questions be asked unself-consciously. And it is contagious.

WHY TALK?

> Any language taught only by adults to adults—or to children as if they were adults—becomes in certain respects "dead". It fails to enlist recruits, it may lose its productivity, and it serves in the end primarily to separate those who know it from those who do not. (Mead, 1959, pp. 143–144)

There is a distinction that must be drawn between a science environment that incorporates child-centered, hands-on methodology, but considers primarily the teacher's questions, and a classroom in which knowledge about science and the world is carefully *co*-constructed, incorporating a child-centered, hands-on methodology that is framed by children's questions. The former represents my work as a science teacher before I began to examine the link between talk and the language of science. Children in my classroom, prior to my work on talk, had varied and rich explorations in science, explorations that I would orchestrate as I provisioned my classroom and encouraged exploratory action and talk focusing on my predetermined questions and assigned tasks.

My goal was to offer them many opportunities to be deeply involved in the stuff of science, to fully explore and act upon those materials while also posing questions that I thought would provoke growth in their thinking. In effect I was always prodding their thinking to go further. Often, however, I was prodding without a clear sense of where "further" was for the children. I knew where I thought their thinking was going, but my ability to assess the real path of that thinking was limited by my own conceptualization of how to direct and guide it. While my students did, in fact, richly construct new understandings of their world, *I did not always richly construct what their under-standings were.*

At some point I began to wonder what children thought about subjects that were not considered to be developmentally appropriate for them. I would eavesdrop on their informal conversations about the universe, about electricity, about the onset of winter, about aging; and I realized that those kinds of topics were missing from my curriculum, but were of deep and intense concern to my students. I perceived that in spite of my prodding, I was not always challenging the children's potential as *thinkers* and their natural ability to consider complex and difficult questions in ways that were useful to them. *I had always been in charge of the questions, asking them and often answering them, and deciding which of the children's questions should be heard.*

Looking More Closely at Language

> The more a learner controls his own language strategies and the more he is enabled to think aloud, the more he can take responsibility for formulating explanatory hypotheses and evaluating them. (Barnes, 1976, p. 29)

Thus, when I began to pursue research on language and literacy, my interest turned to using talk to better understand children's thinking about the world. I was very committed to having children "think out loud" and initiated Science Talks as a way to gather data on the children's questions and their ways of talking about science. Gradually I came in contact with some of the research on classroom discourse (Cazden, 1988; Gee, 1990), on collaborative talk (Barnes, 1976), on narrative (Bruner, 1986; Cazden, John, & Hymes, 1972; Hymes & Cazden, 1980; Wells, 1986). Those works expanded my understanding of talk and fueled a philosophical commitment to it that transformed my practice and re-oriented it.

I learned that what my children were doing as they took over the Science Talks was qualitatively different from what I had orchestrated before the talks. Much to my discomfort I also learned that there was a subtle difference between a child-centered, developmental classroom, where teacher and children construct (usually in a carefully controlled way) knowledge about the world, and a classroom where that process continues but a focus on discourse is added.

In the former classroom, the teacher is in charge of what is said about a subject. The children's remarks are filtered through the teacher's mouth, usually in the form of revoicing and questioning. If there is discussion, the teacher orchestrates it, choosing who talks, what is said, and the most important ideas to be considered and pursued. As Edwards and Mercer (1987) point out, often the most developmentally oriented teaching subtly controls what is said and done, maintaining a basic "power asymmetry" in the classroom. Even in very active learning situations, the notion that students work with their own ideas is "illusory" (pp. 156–158).

Co-Construction of Learning

In a classroom where the appropriation of many different discourses is the goal, the children co-construct, or build together, ideas about seminal questions through real dialogue, and the teacher listens and reflects without immediately agonizing over what *ought* to be said. Instead of intervening in children's discussions at "teachable" moments when children are stating disturbing misconceptions, the teacher begins to focus on issues of language and culture, and wonders how to bridge the gap between her intentions and the child's life experience. Explorations with materials and ideas continue, the commitment to hands-on learning remains, but the teacher's understanding of what she *does not know* about her children rises to the forefront.

I became more and more interested in uncovering children's understandings, and as I did so I realized that too many children brought little or no personal experience to the study of science. While they all had a natural curiosity and interest, few of them understood how the subject fit into their lives. Science was for school, and I (ironically) was the only "scientist" they knew. My sense of responsibility for helping my students place science into the immediate context of their lives grew as I realized that the only way to do that was to uncover their "Stories About Science" (Gallas, 1994), to elicit in any way possible their theories about difficult questions, and to draw very clear connections between their present and future lives and the study of science in school.

As I learned more about language, "co-construction" (Barnes, 1976) was a term that began to fascinate me and showed great potential for children. I had seen how children, when given the opportunity, could use the process of discussion to explore their ideas and construct new ones together. On the one hand, the concept of co-construction was closely related to what I had been doing as a developmental teacher, except that I had been in charge of the "co" part of the co-construction. Although I had been focused on developing children's ideas and encouraging their ability to communicate those ideas, I ago-nized when they consistently would present me with incorrect and bizarre explanations for what they were observing. How could I guide them toward more "correct" conclusions without violating their sense of control over the process of learning?

A closer examination of what happened when children were allowed to collaborate in their thinking without my interference showed me that the process of collaboration had great potential to teach *me* about children's thinking. When I was finally able to be quiet in Science Talks and my students really began to co-construct their ideas together, the outcome was fascinating (see Gallas, 1994). It was as if the eavesdropping I spoke of earlier became formalized, and I could view how their ideas developed, watch theories being built, and be amazed at the power of a group of children thinking together. As time passed (and later chapters will describe), I could even witness where my own teaching had or hadn't been effective.

WHAT IS THE DISCOURSE OF SCIENCE?

> Our discussion is informed by the conviction that a body of practices widely regarded by outsiders as well organized, logical and coherent, in fact consists of a disordered array of observations with which scientists struggle to produce order. Despite participants' well-ordered reconstructions and rationalizations, actual scientific practice entails the confrontations and negotiation of utter confusion. (Latour & Woolgar, 1979, p. 36)

> Ask a scientist what he conceives the scientific method to be and he will adopt an expression that is at once solemn and shifty-eyed: solemn, because he feels he ought to declare an opinion; shifty-eyed because he is wondering how to conceal the fact that he has no opinion to declare. (Medawar, 1982, p. 80)

> Physicists do not start from hypotheses; they start from data. By the time a law has been fixed into an H-D (hypothetico-deductive) system, really original physical thinking is over. (Hanson, 1965, p. 70)

> It is not easy to be sure whether the crucial idea is really one's own or has been unconsciously assimilated in talks with others. (Sir Lawrence Bragg, 1968, p. viii)

As Einstein himself once said, he succeeded in good part because he kept asking himself questions concerning space and time which only children wonder about. (Holton, 1978, p. 279)

Things are much more marvelous than the scientific method allows us to conceive.... *Why* do you know? Why were you so sure of something when you couldn't tell anyone else? You weren't sure in a boastful way; you were sure in what I call a completely internal way.... What you had to do was put it in their frame. So you work with so-called scientific methods to put it into their frame *after* you know. (Barbara McClintock, in Fox-Keller, 1983, p. 203)

What I have found out since I began documenting Science Talks is that the kinds of talk and thinking that children engage in when studying science naturally parallel what both practicing scientists and historians of science report. Children come to school fully prepared to engage in scientific activity, and the school, not recognizing the real nature of scientific thinking and discovery, directs its efforts toward training those natural abilities out of the children. I believe that this process occurs because teachers like myself have never fully experienced or understood what real science is. We have been trained to teach a curriculum without fully exploring both the history of science and the nature of science discourse. Thus our practice as teachers reflects our own flawed education as students of science.

The Process of Science

When I set out to find out what "real" science was, I was fascinated to discover the reasons why I had been so ignorant of the scientific process. Many scientists and historians of science describe how the process of science is completely obscured by the ways in which scientific discoveries are made public. In fact, public impressions of the "scientific method," the isolation of the scientist in his or her laboratory, and the rational nature of scientific discovery are clearly debunked by the accounts of practicing scientists who are willing to discuss their process, by ethnographic studies of laboratory life, and by historical analyses of important work (Beveridge, 1950; Hanson, 1965; Holton, 1973, 1978; Kuhn, 1970; Latour, 1987; Latour & Woolgar, 1979; Lynch, 1985; Medawar, 1982; Watson, 1968).

The Role of Talk

I have learned that the process of scientific discovery is deeply connected to conversation with colleagues, activities that take place both in and out of the laboratory (Latour & Woolgar, 1979; Lynch, 1985). A scientific idea is often the result of many interpersonal exchanges, of interactions with materials, and of false starts. In the end, "facts are socially constructed" (Latour & Woolgar, pp. 169–170). (For an autobiographical account of the pervasiveness of talk in the development of an important scientific discovery, see Watson, 1968.)

Intuition and Imagination

I have also confirmed my long held conviction that the process of scientific discovery is firmly rooted in intuition and imagination (Gallas, 1994). Many accounts of the life work of important scientists confirm that scientists move from a state of deep involvement in the sensation and perception of the unusual in nature toward an articulation of those perceptions. Their initial fascination with a problem originates in childhood wonder and does not proceed toward resolution in a purely logical fashion, but rather combines the processes of creative and critical thinking to produce advances in both the development of theories and the solutions to problems. As Einstein stated: "To these elementary laws there leads no logical path, but only intuition, supported by being sympathetically in touch with experience" (quoted in Holton, 1973, p. 357; see also Cobb, 1994; Fox-Keller, 1983; Hanson, 1965; Holton, 1978; Rothenberg, 1979).

Early Childhood Experiences

Some historians of science have suggested that important events in early childhood often mark a turning point toward fascination with science. Fox-Keller (1983) describes maize geneticist and Nobel Prize winner Barbara McClintock's childhood as representing a deep immersion in, and fascination with, the world of nature, while Holton (1973) cites Einstein's recollection of his first exposure to a magnetic pocket compass at age 4 or 5—an event that provoked his lifelong interest in the mysteries of physics. Holton (1973) calls this memory "an allegory of the formation of the playground of his [Einstein's] basic imagination" (p. 360). In other words, a love of science and the attraction to particular kinds of problems are potentially set into motion in early childhood.

Philosophy and Metaphysics

These fascinations often emerge early and become closely guarded beliefs and preoccupations that continue for a lifetime (Cobb, 1994; Fox-Keller, 1983; Holton, 1978). Holton labels these "thematics," or an individual's theoretical picture of how the world works, and proposes that they form the underpinnings of all scientific work and can account for the development of different schools of thought in a particular field of study. He notes that in the history of science, there are only a few persistent themata, for example, evolution vs. devolution, reductionism vs. holism, hierarchy vs. unity, chaos out of order vs. order from chaos (p. 10); and he postulates that these may emerge even well before an individual becomes a scientist, "in a part of the imagination" (p. 17). A deeply held belief in one of these themata can determine the direction of a scientist's research as well as his or her interpretation of data.

Subjectivity

> And yet, on looking into the history of science, one is overwhelmed by evidences that all too often there is no regular procedure, no logical system of discovery, no simple, continuous development. The process of discovery has been as varied as the temperament of the scientist. (Holton, 1973, pp. 384–385)

Each scientist brings her or his own very subjective lens through which to examine a question. In fact, the separation of the subjective, personal vision of a scientist and the more objective world of "real" science is not, as some critics of modern science propose, as clear-cut as most of us believe (Edelglass, Maier, Gebert, & Davy, 1992). Because most of our knowledge of science is communicated to us as finished and accepted facts or theories, that is, as "final form presentation of science" (Duschl, 1990, p. 68), we do not have any knowledge of the process of "private science," which is influenced and bounded by social, intellectual, metaphysical, and creative processes that most of us would believe to be quite "unscientific" (Fox-Keller, 1983; Rothenberg, 1979).

Thus, in examining the world of the scientist, I find that the interpersonal—that is, talk and the laboratory—is linked with ideas that emerge from the purely personal playground of imagination and wonder. The very private musing of a child finds its origins in wonder and may eventually be transformed through reflection, dialogue, and finally collaboration into a question and ultimately a theory about the world. These are the seeds that the classroom can nurture and build upon as teachers and children mutually engage in the world of science.

CHAPTER 2

Science Talks: An Overview

VERA: Yeah but my question is . . . why should ice float, if, if water sinks, because ice, ice, you see, if we put some water on a scale, and then ice, what would the water weigh? It would hardly weigh anything, and if we put ice on the scale, it would weigh something. But, but then why would it not, why does water sink and if it doesn't it won't weigh anything? And why would

DANNY: Uh, Vera?

VERA: ice float if it does weigh something?

DANNY: Um. How would we, um,

CHLOE: If you put it in something, then it will make it heavier.

VERA: You could try a scale. Oh, I know, I think I know! Maybe it's the amount of water, maybe it's the amount of water that made it heavier, and, the

DANNY: Vera?

VERA: the ice, the, um, and there was a little bit of ice and there was more water than the ice.

OLLIE: Vera?

VERA: Yeah?

ROBERTO: There is a way. There is a way to weigh water, like Mr. P. said. He took a piece of tape, and he writed it. He made numbers on it so there is a way to weigh water. Vera is right.

ARI: Or you could put it on a scale.

T: Or you could put it on a scale.

VERA: Or you could *pour it* on a scale? Or you could pour, um, a bucket of water onto a scale . . . but I doubt my mom and dad would let me do that.

—Excerpt from the Science Talk: *"Why does ice float?"*—Grade 1

For my class, Science Talks emerged as a type of discussion in the fall of 1989. At that time I initiated the talks in my first grade classroom based on my long-term observations that the most exciting science discussions took place informally, outside of my teaching role. I originally had intended the discussions to be child-centered, with little if any direction from me. What I hoped to discover was the young child's natural style of talking about the world. It was, one might say, a naive and fairly unconstructed piece of research, but it quite adequately represented the style of teacher research that has characterized my practice. What I had was a question and some undocumented knowledge that children were far more sophisticated and able to think about difficult questions than my training in cognitive science had led me to believe. Thus, I began with a question and a hunch, and the style of Science Talks was conceived.

Since the first year of talks in 1989, I have witnessed more than 100 Science Talks with both first and second graders in my own classroom, as well as with classes of third and fifth graders. Those children and other teachers have taught me that the effect of Science Talks is consistent across the grades. For children, there is an immediate sense of the importance of the discussions. When their teachers and I ask them what questions they would like to talk about, and we proceed week by week to set time aside for discussions in which we are not the leaders or the experts, the children begin to work hard at talking to each other, much as the children did in the excerpt that opened this chapter.

For teachers, the talks always provide a surprise. Sometimes, as in this excerpt, what is striking is the tenacity of a child like Vera's effort to talk through an idea. Or it may be the care with which the other children responded to and tried to assist her, or it may be simply taking delight in the unbounded enthusiasm and ingenuousness Vera portrayed when she suggested pouring the water on a scale and then decided, "I doubt my mom and dad would let me do that." On some level, these talks enable teachers to see their students with fresh eyes, to savor their intelligence and deep enthusiasm for a question.

Yet I, and most teachers who have tried this kind of talk, are never prepared for the distress we feel when we find we have to be quiet. It is the teacher's way to want to facilitate discussion; to moderate who talks and for how long; to discourage what I call bird walks, or digressions that seem to be off the topic; to make sure that children finally get the right answer (if it's a known one). When children eagerly begin to co-construct theories, when their exploratory talk wanders so broadly and quickly that we can't follow it, we make an assumption that the talks are out of control.

For many teachers, and this was absolutely true for me, the process of hearing an audiotape of the first talk and realizing how dominant our voices are even when we are trying *not* to control the talks, is daunting. The act of giving up overt control of the talks takes time and determination, and is almost painful. One must trust that the act of talking about a question is an opening for much richer scientific explorations. The reward, however, is the ability to watch and document the natural unfolding of dialogue among children, to see a class of children begin to think in concert, and to witness the power and deep intelligence they have as individuals and as a group.

INTRODUCING THE TALKS

I began our first Science Talk with a focusing question, one that I still use every year with each new class because it illustrates the nature of the questions we will consider. "Why do the leaves change color?" I ask each fall, and just as in the first year I am continuously astonished by the enthusiasm and originality of the children's theories and the eagerness with which they adopt the talks as their own.

"Why do the leaves change color?" —October 1991—Grade 1

TOM: It gets colder and all the green comes out of 'em, and all the brown, it takes all the wh—
?: the juice
TOM: it takes all the juice out of 'em that the caterpillars eat.
T: Oh, so it takes all the juice that the caterpillars eat. . . . You don't think that?
?: Karen, Karen.
T: Go ahead, Ellen. Listen to her and she'll give you an idea.
ELLEN: Because I, I don't think caterpillars could drink that much juice 'cause trees have a lot.
TOM: No, they eat the leaves. And the juice goes into them, and they grow bigger and bigger and get into a cocoon so their skin peels off.
T: You don't agree with that? Why don't you agree with that?
TOM: I don't agree with what she said.
T: She hasn't even said anything. Tom, in Science Talks the purpose is not that each person is the best science talker. The purpose of Science Talks is that you begin to talk *with* your friends and figure it out together.
ELLEN: I don't know . . .
T: What do you think? Everybody may not know.

ELLEN: I think the sap runs out.
T: You think the sap runs out?
ELLEN: Of the leaves. 'Cause it goes, 'cause it goes, 'cause leaves
        sweat like we do.
T: Yes, leaves sweat like we do. Water comes out of them.

As I noted earlier, I generally introduce Science Talks in early
October and describe them to the children as a time when they can
speak with each other about important questions. As an introduction,
I propose a question that is completely open ended and whose answer
will most probably be unknown to children of their age. In the first
talk, we sit in a circle together, and I establish one rule: *You don't have
to raise your hand.* I need that rule, because it is important that I, as the
teacher, am not seen as the moderator of the discussions. I also do two
things in the early talks. First, as the above excerpt shows, I try to show
how to listen and how to recognize each child who wants to participate. That is both a verbal and and nonverbal kind of modeling. In
other words, in the excerpt above I responded to Ellen's remark by
saying out loud what I might have said in my head to make sense of
her statement.

ELLEN: 'cause leaves sweat like we do.
T: Yes, leaves sweat like we do. Water comes out of them.

And at the same time I acknowledge Ellen's nonverbal response (shak-
ing her head "no") to Tom's early remark by turning my body toward
her and urging her to say what she's thinking: "You don't think that?. . .
Go ahead. . ."
      Sometimes, as with Tom in this discussion, I provide very explicit
information about what distinguishes these kinds of talks from other
situations: "The purpose is not that each person is the best science
talker." I am both coaching him as to what his goals might be for the
talk and establishing a protocol. In other words, I am telling Tom not
to intimidate other children by being verbally combative, something
that characterized much of his interactions in the early part of first
grade.
      In order to keep track of participation for our follow-up discus-
sion, and for my long-term records, I also tape record the talk (see
Appendix B for full transcripts) and take field notes, recording, for
example, who spoke; what previous idea, if any, they referred to; explicit examples of silent children whose body language indicated at-
tentiveness to the process; descriptions of the development of theories,

and so forth. The following excerpt from my field notes shows the kinds of observations I might make. (Note that brackets indicate my interpretations of different events, or reminders to myself.)

Field Notes: March 23, 1994—*"How do plants grow?"*

This is a question Cindy has framed to support her unit on growth. Germaine starts out with a very practical statement on how to plant a seed. Maurice repeats it. Michael asks to clarify the question. Dierdre asks a super question in response to Michael's, and it's a beauty! [Check that one out on the tape.] Michael says, "What about the pumpkin seed? It sprouted without dirt in the sink." [Conditions for growth: Evidence from their own experience. Note new talk/science behaviors here: 1. Asking for clarification of their assertions. (See Mia on tape.) 2. Nate asks Tian to "define 'nutrition,'" meaning "define your terms." This is a trend we started with the *Gravity* talk when I asked Michael to define "gravity." 3. Questions are leading to more questions of greater complexity.] Germaine is getting *so* clear in how he forms his questions. He really uses "maybe." This talk keeps going back to the question, "How did plants begin?" Eli tells me that that should have been the "original question." At the end, Germaine says, "I have a question. True or false, do plants grow best in water?" [Wow! Fantastic! He is truly honing in on what this science stuff is!]

In early Science Talks, not all children talk, but there is usually a core who try to say something, a group that is silent, but very attentive, and a small number who are either uncomfortable or feign disinterest. (The latter kinds of children will be discussed later in this chapter.)

The first talk usually lasts about 15–20 minutes and is followed by a brainstorming session of more questions. We also talk briefly about how the talk went, and from my field notes I make very explicit comments about the kinds of things I saw that let me know someone was really listening and thinking about the statements of others: body language, eye contact, references to prior statements, and questioning; for example:

T: There were some really good ideas here. People came up with really good things, and if you were thinking silently in your head, that's fine too, because I know. I could see everybody was thinking and their brains were going. So, for people who spoke and told us your ideas out loud, they were good ones. For people who were thinking, think some more about it. See what you, see what you come up with.

However, I do not establish any firm rules for the talks beyond the "you don't have to raise your hand" rule. Each group and age of science talkers is different, and the kinds of rules and interventions that facilitate the talks differ from class to class (see Chapter 9 for further explanation of the teacher's role as coach and model).

WHO OWNS THE TALKS?

One spring, my student teacher, who was conducting a unit on seeds, scheduled a Science Talk and told the children she wanted them to talk about her question. There was an immediate uproar. "You can't ask a question," a child retorted, "these are our talks!" The student teacher was stunned, but persisted by explaining that she didn't want to take over the talks, only to find out what they thought about her question. The children very graciously relented, but this incident underscored the issue of ownership of this forum.

When I initiated the talks, my intention was to establish a regular structure where the children's ideas and questions would predominate. In the first year, I never proposed a question of my own, but in the spring of that year, I witnessed a talk on the question, "What makes the wind?" which I followed by a read aloud experience from a book of the same name I happened to find. Two weeks later, I followed up with a second talk on the same question to ascertain the impact of the book. Because this question is not one that is normally considered in a first grade science curriculum, it was an unusual opportunity to see whether changes had taken place in the children's thinking as a result of the original discussion and the reading of the book. Within this second discussion I observed that not only had every child understood how wind was made, but they were able to move beyond the original question to consider two more difficult ideas: how tornadoes are made, and how air circulation affects weather patterns.

It was clear to me that the first discussion had focused the children's thinking on the question and had created a readiness for new information. I saw at that point that the Science Talks could provide a powerful tool for me to use as a teacher. The following year I began to judiciously insert questions of my own at times when we were about to begin a unit of study. I have found that a discussion of my question prior to a unit of study prepares the children for consideration of new ideas. It also enables me to assess the kinds of knowledge they bring to their work. (Chapters 5, 6, and 8 will expand on consideration of both the importance of identifying seminal questions prior to a unit of study, and how children's misconceptions are revealed through the talks.)

In this way the ownership of the talks expanded. My students are now much more comfortable with my occasional use of the talks for my own purposes. However, there is a further issue of ownership that relates to participation by the children. Science Talks enable new voices to emerge as authoritative because the hierarchy of the classroom is blurred when the teacher moves out of an authoritative role. I have found as I have worked with my own classes and with other teachers that the open ended format of the talks allows children who are not high achievers to show that they are keen observers of the world and powerful creative thinkers. In effect, the Science Talks, by considering questions whose answers are not known, invite every child to participate. The process of constructing an answer with others, of using everything that's been observed and imagined, stimulates more participation in science than a recitation of information from a book.

I also am often surprised at the long periods of silence maintained by those children who are not able to participate in the talks. Obviously, some of those children are inordinately shy and need a very long time to truly believe that every idea will be thoughtfully considered. My active presence as a listener and archivist guarantees that each child will be respectfully heard, although some classes need quite pointed work in how to listen to others. (Chapter 9 will discuss that kind of challenge in more depth.) Shy children, however, are usually very present as listeners, following the discussions carefully with many nonverbal signs of participation and interest. Eventually, most of them do attempt to participate.

In my experience, however, the most striking nonparticipants are the children who one would most expect to delight in these talks, and those are the high achieving, highly verbal, information-oriented children (usually boys), who normally stand out in teacher-led discussions and in child-centered explorations of materials.

Donald is that kind of child. He entered school with an extraordinary amount of memorized book knowledge about science. He had the kind of information about space, animals, and plants that normally astonishes adults and leads them to pronounce that such a child is gifted and precocious for his years. Soon after entering school, Donald was recognized by his first grade class as the science expert. His love of the natural world, his library of books, and his accounts of family excursions on weekends provided rich information for us all.

However, I soon observed in my field notes that in first grade Donald rarely participated in Science Talks. He would remain silent during the talks, and, further, he was inattentive to the other children's ideas, trying to engage his friends in whispering and pranks while they were listening, and very clearly indicating with his body language that he didn't want to participate. When I noticed this, I began to ask Donald outside of the talks why he was quiet. Did he know the answers to the questions? He said that he didn't know the answers either, but that he just couldn't think what to say.

His silence continued throughout the year, with a few exceptions of talks in which he had some information. I noted in my field notes in late March, during a talk on "What makes colors in nature?":

> This is a very raucous discussion. I notice that all the children are participating except for Donald, our most knowledgeable science buff. I realize that he never speaks in a Science Talk unless he has had prior information on the topic. He is unable to engage on this one. I wonder if too much prior knowledge makes you less able to work on open ended questions. In some ways these talks make a level playing field. All children can participate and build plausible theories.

Later in April, my notes record this observation during the talk, *"Does the universe end?"*

> Donald entered this discussion first to clarify the question and then to make an extensive display of knowledge. He spoke in very quick spurts, like he was reading from a book, kind of a staccato delivery of facts, "'cause the sun'll burn, and the sun will be a white dwarf, 'cause the sun's a star, and then, um, the earth'll burn, and we'll freeze." Later in the talk, Donald forcefully rebutted Katie's mix-up of the words "universe" and "solar system." His vocal intonation was very high pitched, authoritative, and impatient: "The universe is the whole space. The solar system, the milky way, our solar system and there's other solar systems to other planets. . . . First of all, there's not only one solar sys-

tem, and second of all, the solar system is in the universe,
so how can it be bigger than the universe?"

The pattern that seemed to be emerging that first year, was that Donald
would participate only when there was no risk in joining us because
he could display his knowledge, and when he did say something the
tone of his remarks was always intimidating.

His pattern is one that I've observed in a few other boys who also
hold back from participating in the talks. Perhaps the talks violate their
sense of what science is. In other words, they have been prepared before entering school to feel "scientific." For them, science is like saving
money in a bank: Acquire an extraordinary amount of information,
and that makes you scientific. However, Science Talks, as I noted in
my field notes, create a level playing field. Everyone can be scientific,
even the least privileged children in the class, and everyone has important questions that provoke energetic discussion.

ABOUT THE QUESTIONS

True dialogue occurs when teachers ask questions to which they
do not presume to already know the correct answer. (Lemke,
1990, p. 55)

The questions that work best for Science Talks, whether posed by
teachers or children, are those that are open ended with the possibility
of many answers. Initially, some children ask questions that have a very
specific answer, for example, "Who made the first clock?" Based on
my experience with other classes and other teachers, I have two frames
of thought on whether this kind of question should be discussed.
Clearly, if this discussion is held, the children soon find that first there
is only one answer and if one of them knows it the discussion quickly
ends, and second if no one knows the answer the discussion turns into
an argument about whether it is possible to determine a correct answer. For some classes of children, particularly in the older grades,
teachers have found that it is instructive to let them try that kind of
talk, and then discuss what kinds of questions are most useful for developing dialogue. My experience with younger children is that they
don't ask as many closed questions, and when they do, it is not always
helpful to discuss the questions and why they don't work.

Recently, in working with a class of children that had trouble talking together (see Chapter 9), I learned that questions need to be care-

fully phrased so that all children are able to understand the context of the discussion. In other words, if a child asks, "What is gravity?" only those children who are familiar with the term "gravity" can speak about the question. (And often, an ability to refer to the word does not imply an understanding of it.) However, there are ways to rephrase the question so that all children can participate in a discussion about the effects of gravity. For example, that question could be rephrased, "Why, when we throw a ball up in the air, does it come back down?" Sometimes what we interpret as uninterested silence, or lack of information on the part of a nonparticipating child, is really a misunderstanding of a question. When the question is rephrased, many children will exclaim, "So that's what you meant!"

Most children, however, ask questions that are simply phrased and either are based on observations of a natural phenomenon or are "big picture" questions. For example, after feeding our cockatiels sunflower seeds each day for more than 6 months, Andy asked the question, "Why don't birds have teeth?" based on his close observation of how the cockatiels cracked and then ate the seeds. That question provoked a rich Science Talk in which the children used very detailed observations of our birds and of other birds they had noticed in nature as well as book knowledge to construct, not an answer to the question, but a theory as to *how* birds ate without teeth. The "why" of Andy's question was saved for a later talk, after we had done further research and observation on the "how." Yet his question was posed in a very practical way that all children would want to discuss, and it prompted a series of rich inquiries by the class.

Another child, in studying birds, might ask a big picture question about birds, for example, "How did birds begin?" That question, although a difficult and confounding one, is one that many children ask as they watch birds in nature or in captivity and wonder about their evolution. In both cases the questions are worded simply and directly, and in tracking children's questions, I have learned to consider how I phrase questions for my teaching, monitoring both the simplicity of the question and the kinds of language I use.

VIEWING CHILDREN'S KNOWLEDGE

Making explicit the arguments underlying conceptual ambitions
and dissatisfactions, ... we bring to light ... the particular picture of
human beings as active intelligences. (Toulmin, 1972, p. 3)

Toulmin, in describing what he terms an "epistemic self-portrait," proposes that human knowledge must be considered from two vantage points: We need to understand what we believe in, and then we need to analyze the bases on which we anchor those beliefs. The process of Science Talks enables children and their teachers to see each child's epistemic self-portrait and then to pursue the origins and reasoning that support his or her position.

For example, Ellen and Tom have two very similar explanations for why the leaves turn colors. Tom believes, "It gets colder and all the green comes out of 'em. . . . It takes all the juice that the caterpillars eat." Ellen thinks, "The sap runs out. . . . Of the leaves . . . 'cause leaves sweat like we do." Their beliefs are similar, but based on different observations. Tom relates the change to a change in weather and the activity of caterpillars, while Ellen makes an analogy between our sweat and the respiration of leaves. Both children have observed the process and combined that observation with their respective knowledge of nature. Tom, an avid naturalist who specializes in collecting and caring for little creatures such as caterpillars, constructs a theory based on his knowledge of those larvae. Ellen, who is more bookish and a precocious reader, juxtaposes her book facts with her observations of her own loss of fluids and constructs a theory that is similar to Tom's, but distinctly different in its point of origin. Both children enable me to view the origin and structure of their ideas, and to shape my teaching response accordingly.

However, in addition to discovering each child's system of reasoning, Science Talks also enable me to observe children employing overarching beliefs as a basis for building their arguments, what Holton (1978) termed "themata" in his study of the history of science. Over the course of a year particular children might base most of their theories about a variety of questions on one pervasive idea. For example, a child who believes that the origin of all natural phenomena is found in one source, might cite "germs" or "chemicals" as causal agents for almost every seminal event in the earth's natural history from the beginning of the earth to the development of grasses. Other children might believe that the universe is random and disorderly, and therefore that events of any kind are not predictable. Still others believe the universe is supremely ordered and all events are interrelated.

The children who speak in this book often display this characteristic, which Holton describes as consistent in the work of most scientists. Borrowing from Holton's (1978) schemata for how thematics work in the scientific mind (p. 8), experiences that children have in nature enable them to develop propositions about how nature works. Those ex-

Figure 2.1 Two Theories About Why Leaves Turn Color

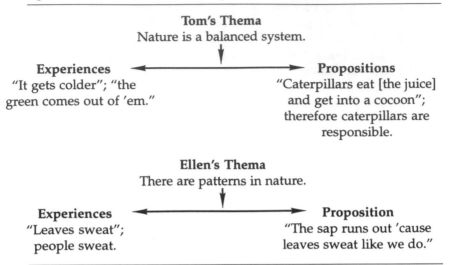

Tom's Thema
Nature is a balanced system.

Experiences   **Propositions**
"It gets colder"; "the   "Caterpillars eat [the juice]
green comes out of 'em."   and get into a cocoon";
                                        therefore caterpillars are
                                        responsible.

Ellen's Thema
There are patterns in nature.

Experiences   **Proposition**
"Leaves sweat";   "The sap runs out 'cause
people sweat.   leaves sweat like we do."

periences and propositions, however, are mediated by the child's beliefs and convictions about the world. Using this structure, I might picture Tom's and Ellen's themata about this question as shown in Figure 2.1.

If I view a child's theory, or epistemic self-portrait, from this position, I can see that the immediate statement the child makes about nature begins with observations or book facts and proceeds toward the statement of a proposition or theory. Running through that seemingly logical progression, however, and influencing it at all stages, are the underlying themata that Holton would maintain are the underpinnings that determine both the form and the content of most scientific theories. These ideas spring from the realm of imagination, intuition, and metaphysics, and are governed by deeply held beliefs about the world.

By examining the structure of children's thinking in Science Talks, I can trace the logic and consistency of their ideas, rather than focusing on their *incorrect* information or concepts. Further, when children put their ideas out on the floor as part of our discussion, they are showing a willingness to have those ideas discussed, and perhaps modified, if they are incorrect.

Alan, for example, after watching an annular eclipse out on the school lawn for more than 2 hours, developed a magical theory about why the eclipse occurred. The following Science Talk about the question, "Why did the eclipse happen?" took place the next day:

ALAN: Well, I think that, um, uh, the eclipse happens. But maybe it
    happens every few times. I'm not sure, but maybe it did some-
    thing to the earth. And the eclipse makes *it* come, and then it
    wears away. The next, whatever, 14 years, it comes back, to, um,
    the things come back so it won't go away completely.

Maurice tried to help Alan clarify his statement.

MAURICE: Do you mean there's a . . . plants are starting to get too
    hot, and then the eclipse comes back, and they cool down?
ALAN: Maybe it's a sign for something.

As the children worked with Alan to help him say more, I realized that
he had developed a very elaborate, imaginative, and deeply personal
explanation for the phenomenon of the eclipse: The eclipse happened
in response to a need from the earth. In Alan's mind, the earth told the
sun that it needed something, and the eclipse was the result.

Thus, in the process of talking science, as the child describes his
or her beliefs behind a theory, considers new ideas, and has old ones
challenged, both child and teacher can see a more complete epistemic
self-portrait. Until children's ideas are publicly articulated, neither
teacher nor child can consider their meaning and validity. Once ideas
have been stated, both child and teacher know where to begin their
dialogue about a question, and the teacher can develop experiences
that help the child think further about a question. (Chapters 4 and 6
will examine the issue of epistemics and themata further.)

LEARNING TO TALK TOGETHER

VERA: Well, Anita hasn't got the point, I think, because if ice was
    colder than water, what does that have to do with making it
    float?
ANITA: But it's not freezing when it's colder when you hold it in your
    hand.
VERA: Yeah, but what does that have . . . you know. . . . Well then,
    why do we have, then why, that has nothing to do with what
    we're talking about 'cause why, if this ice was cold, why would
    that make it float, even if, why, what does that make, why would
    that make it float if it was, just if it was, if it was cold, what does
    that make it float? What does that make, what does that have to
    do with making it float? I don't understand.
T: Coldness?
CHLOE: Al, what does it have to do with being both tasting good?

ROBERTO: Um, Vera? One more thing. Bet my sister could figure this out.

VERA: Um, Roberto, please!

DAN: This has nothing to do with . . .

OLLIE: We're not talking about your sister, Roberto.

VERA: This is a, this is a 1-G [name of our class] science thing. Now let's get back to what we were talking about. Now Roberto,

ROBERTO: My sister *can* find it out because she goes to science practice.

DAN: Roberto . . . This is nothing about . . . this is nothing about your sister, Roberto.

ROBERTO: And, but it is science, and she knows about science. She can actually figure this out. If I *had* her.

T: Well maybe you could go ask her. Go ask her. Next time you see her, Roberto, go ask her for us.

DAN: He'll see her coming, coming to pick him up, I bet.

JOHN: And then, just, bring her the paper out, and tell her to write it down, 'cause you can't remember it.

During the year, a class of children grows in its ability to talk together and build acceptable theories. If Science Talks are held regularly, once every 1 or 2 weeks, ways of co-constructing knowledge spill over into other areas of the curriculum, and the sophistication of all classroom discussions increases. Further, as a teacher who had to learn to be quiet in Science Talks, my ability to listen and understand children's utterances improves over time.

As the talks progress, I continue to coach the children on ways to make their talks more effective: how to use each other's ideas and support new theories, how to ask clarifying questions and apply prior knowledge. Often there are children in the class who do this naturally. One might say that their dialogic intelligence is already well developed, and they very consciously help discussions move forward. But essentially Science Talks become an invaluable tool for all of us to learn how to discuss and think together.

For myself, the talks open a window into the children's thinking from which I can see their early ideas on many topics, as well as providing me with a view of their deep interests and topics I can pursue in my science curriculum. Often, in the midst of a unit of study, a child will pose a new question that propels our work forward to new and unexpected levels and refines our dialogue about a subject. Thus, Science Talks become a forum where children can introduce new tangents of thought into our ongoing science curriculum. The children seem to know that this is a way to put an idea on the floor. They also know that public questions and statements become food for thought for everyone in the class and that one person's question can become everyone's burning fascination. The talks support their growing sense of what science is, of what kinds of ideas science considers, and of how it feels to speak with authority and seriousness about difficult questions.

CHAPTER 3

Anatomy of a Science Talk

> The struggle to share their thinking forces a collaborative explic-
> itness upon the group. Elaboration of language is not just a matter
> of each child's language habits, but can be fostered by a group's striv-
> ing to think aloud together. (Barnes, 1976, p. 45)

In this chapter, I would like to dismantle the talks. That is, I hope to show what the underlying structure of a talk would look like if it were to be placed in a semantic map. This exercise will accomplish two things: First, it will explicate the logic and consistency of the children's efforts, in effect illustrating that what often *sounds* chaotic to an inexperienced listener, is very purposeful. (As I stated in Chapter 2, these talks are initially very disconcerting for teachers. We cannot hear the sense of the discussion; neither can we follow the very rapid and deft connections the children are making.) Second, it will underscore the kinds of talk behaviors first and second graders often employ without any teacher direction. I believe it is tremendously important for adults who work with children to develop ways to listen to children. In this case, we can listen for ideas, and we can also listen for the structures children use to present their ideas.

HOW DID RICE PLANTS BEGIN?

This question was proposed by a first grade girl in the middle of a unit on the life cycle of plants, which is a curriculum topic for first graders in my school system. The question arose both from the concept of life cycles and from our efforts to sprout and grow rice in our Gro-Lab. (The Gro-Lab is a planting unit that has been designed by the National Gardening Association for classroom use. It consists of two levels of wide trays lit by artificial lights and enclosed by plastic curtains. In my classroom, which has no natural light, the unit allows me to carry out planting activities all year round.)

Because many of my students are of Asian origins, we had become very interested in seeing if we would have any success growing rice indoors. Hence, the question emerged from prior knowledge about life cycles and the importance of the seed, from an understanding of the importance of rice as a food staple in another culture, and from a curiosity as to how such a plant evolved. (Many of the questions children ask about science are focused on the "origins" of things, a topic that will be discussed more in Chapter 6.)

I am using this particular talk because it occurred late in the school year, and the children had had at least 8 months of science talking experience. Therefore the talk illustrates what is possible for more experienced talkers: how collaborative and exploratory talk naturally occur and the potential of very young children to build new theories based on past and newly acquired knowledge. These children ranged in age from 6 to 8 years, and participation was equally distributed among the ages.

CONTENT OF THE TALK

For the purposes of summarizing the talk, I will use the children's text to describe the progression of ideas, and follow this description with a closer look at the development of the talk and the strategies the children used.

Initially, Ellen clarified the question for us.

T: The question was . . . what was the question, Ellen? What came first? Rice or plant?
ELLEN: No. How did rice begin life? How did a plant begin? What made the seed?

Molly proposed an initial idea that was followed by several attempts to build a theory.

MOLLY: Maybe it started out with a kind of grass, like humans started out as animals and it got more like rice.
JOHN: Humans did start as animals.
SHELLY: Yeah, life started with grass 'cause rice is like a grass.
ELLEN: I know 'cause grass seeds start turning sort of like ricey.
JOHN: In the beginning, before people, we were monkeys.
VOICES: Yeah . . . kind of like people to apes . . . yeah.
SHELLY: You know how rice is a plant? And it's also a grass. So the

grass . . . the seed from the grass, um, would drop off and some
may blow away and then there would be more and more. But
you can't do anything to rice. Spray it, or else it probably won't
grow. It will turn moldy like.

Shelly's comment, which attempts to summarize the initial idea but
tapers off into a tangent, is followed by a silence of a full minute. As
often happens with long silences that signal the question is very hard,
I restart the discussion by referring to a prior comment, in this case
Molly's opening idea that rice may have started out as something else:
"a kind of grass." Allen picks up the talk again, and states a new addition to the first idea.

ALLEN: Maybe it's something like, maybe like a sort of germ is float-
    ing in the air, and it lands on grasses, and, which, um, which
    made them turn into rice, um, and then the rice spread, like
    when the wind came the rice would spread, and um, maybe
    that's how it started growing.

Other children, however, are still trying to make the rice to grass connection and don't immediately follow up on Allen's idea.

ELLEN: I'm thinking of something else. Um, I've seen grass that looks
    a little like a rice plant but it, like, was much littler.
BRANDY: I've seen grass that looked like a rice plant, only it wasn't
    grass though, it was a bulb.

Then, seeming to have accepted the jump from rice to grass, Brandy
and the other children begin to expand and develop Allen's contri-
bution.

BRANDY: I think maybe a special kind of seed that got, that got made
    in dirt, the dirt, it made it kind of sprout into rice.
SHELLY: Yeah I thought . . . I started to say that but I, I wasn't exactly
    saying the same thing though. I was saying more like . . . the
    rice, um . . . well, the grass dropped its seeds and then, it flew in
    the air and landed in dirt and then it developed.

Molly asks for clarification.

MOLLY: I don't understand how that works.
BRANDY: Well, maybe a special kind of dirt, a long time ago that we

don't have anymore, maybe just got mixed with all kinds of chemicals or something like that . . . well sort of like what Shelly said about turning into that.

The children have begun to try to explain how a grass might transform into rice by incorporating the "germ" or "chemical" idea. These terms often run throughout many discussions when the origins of an event are being explored. Paul, however, is not convinced of the application of the germ idea to this situation, seeing the connections of germ or chemical and the grass seed as too unpredictable, and he asks for more concrete examples.

PAUL: I sort of agree with Allen except um, would it be a big field like, but what if it was the size of our field [the playground], wouldn't it fall on like, something else. Wouldn't there be, like, rocks in the way?
ALLEN: Well, um, well, maybe it was attracted to, um, grass in a way, or something like that, um, and, and, and maybe once it landed on something, it, um, some, some of the chemicals, just some of it might, um, land on the, um, land on the grass, and then, like, the rest of it would detach and go onto another one.

Paul's request for more details triggered a movement in the talk, one that required Allen to slip into a very hypothetical mode of thought. Allen incorporated Brandy's adaptation of "germ" to "chemical" and attempted to respond. His halting speech signaled the movement into a completely hypothetical mode, and when he finished speaking there was another long silence as we all thought about what he had said. His response to Paul suggested that a mysterious recombination of elements might have occurred in the change from grass to rice. Clearly, Allen developed the idea as he talked, and it was so vague that it required the listeners also to adopt a very loose and hypothetical attitude in order to follow him. Allen's willingness to think out loud *eventually* moved the discussion forward.

However, when the silence was broken, again at my intervention, I asked a question that diverted the children from Allen's explanation. At this point in the talk I was still interested in having the children make the connection with evolution that they had initiated in the first part of the talk, and so, without perceiving that, in fact, Allen's idea was building on that connection, I tried to steer them backwards.

T: This is like two different sort of ideas. Do you think . . . let me ask you a question, 'cause some people said, well, it's kind of like people turning into humans from apes. Do you think the same thing has happened to us, that something went in the air and caused us to change?

The children immediately rejected that comparison, but were diverted to a renewed discussion of evolution that temporarily distracted them.

?: No.
TONY: No. Those are just for plants.
SHELLY: 'Cause we're not plants.
JOHN: Over the years we started to change.
T: They're kind of related.
SHELLY: But we're not plants.
JOHN: People ate different things, and maybe they started to change.

Eventually Brandy moved the group back on track.

BRANDY: We're not talking about apes anymore.
SHELLY: Like rice couldn't eat something. It could have a lot of water.
     Rice could have water. Rice could have water. They don't eat dirt.
ANDY: Plants will eat anything that's a chemical.
T: OK, so it's back to the chemicals.

And the children return to Allen's difficult, but provocative, proposal, still trying to please me by continuing their idea of how "eating" might have influenced evolution, but attempting also to work out how a chemical mixing might have changed the size or shape of a grass. Once again, Paul is skeptical and suggests that their focus on grass might be wrong.

PAUL: Maybe it wasn't the grass, it was another thing.
T: Maybe it wasn't the grass?
?: Yeah, it could have been a leaf.
ANDY: Maybe it was a tree.
SHELLY: No, I don't think so.
?: A tree?
JOHN: A baby tree?
ANDY: I never saw, I never saw a rice, and I'm thinking it looks the
     same as wheat.

Andy's effort to find another plant that rice might resemble refocused the group.

MOLLY: Andy gave me an idea. It could have been, like, wheat changed into rice. Or maybe it was something like, like some different seeds, like, got blown together and then they mixed, and then fell onto the ground.

Molly, the original proponent of the relationship between rice and grass, picks up Andy's idea and attempts to combine it with Brandy's notion of "mixing" and Allen's picture of being "attracted" to other seeds. Molly elaborated:

MOLLY: Maybe like, it was, like, just for an example, when some wheat seeds and some grass seeds got blown up together, when the wind was blowing them, and then, they like hit each other and fell to the ground and they, the roots got tangled up together so they formed a different plant.

The metaphor of a recombination is continued, but the other children reject Molly's incorrect notion that new plants grow from tangled roots.

ELLEN: I have a question about your idea, Molly. How could they . . .
    I thought they were seeds, not plants.

In the process of a vociferous correction of that idea, many voices broke out in excitement. The tape at this point recorded so much concurrent talk that it was impossible to transcribe, but cacophony in the Science Talks always signals that a break is going to be made in the children's thinking. Although Molly had made an incorrect statement, her further elaboration of Allen's and Brandy's ideas, and her changing of Allen's vague use of the word "attracted to" to "blown" (a term Shelly had used in the first minute of that talk: "So the grass . . . the seed from the grass would drop off and some may blow away"), triggered the next leap of thought, and that is what produced the rush of voices.
    At that point I heard a faint voice in the background talking about flowers, and I saw that at least one child was making a connection that I had not expected to hear.

T: Brandy, what did you say?
BRANDY: Maybe it was a flower.
T: Can you talk a little bit about how the flowers, what might have happened.

BRANDY: Maybe it was, like, a special kind of flower, and it *was* a special kind of flower, and it was like a rice flower.
T: So, could flowers have mixed up instead of seeds?
SHELLY: Yeah! The pollen! Pollen!

And so the group moved from Molly's first association of grass with rice and connected that original idea with their recently acquired knowledge of how flowers form seeds.

However, as can be seen from this description of the talk, the outcome resulted from the children's willingness to co-construct and connect a series of theories, many of which contained the genesis of later ideas. One also can see that, although in the final stage of the talk my participation pushed the children to make the last important connection, early in the talk my inability to follow the ideas as well as they did temporarily diverted them from their process. Even in writing this, and trying to expose carefully the linkages between their ideas, I am better able to see how carefully they listen to one another and how the ideas that seem to pop out of midair at the end of a talk are actually very carefully and logically co-constructed from beginning to end.

LOOKING MORE CLOSELY AT TALK BEHAVIORS

The way that this talk unfolded is typical of most Science Talks. Generally the talks follow a process in which a theory is proposed, children make attempts to support it through analogy or fact, clarifying questions are asked, and the theory is revised or expanded. As Figure 3.1 illustrates, this is a dynamic process that repeats itself throughout the discussion. Within each of these phases of development, there are certain phrases, or kinds of thinking, that stand out. The attempts to pose a theory are usually marked by the phrase "Maybe" or are posited in a tentative tone. The children learn that in proposing an idea, they should be careful not to adopt an authoritative voice. For example, in my field notes from October 1992, a second grader very explicitly gave instruction to a new first grade science talker, objecting to his style of always asserting truth: "You should say 'maybe' before you try to answer the question." In other words, it's bad talk to speak with finality if you are trying to have a dialogue. This is not something I have taught the children. It is a talk behavior they have shown me and teach each other.

Support for an idea is made in the form of a statement, either of prior knowledge such as Shelly's assertion, "Rice is like a grass," or

Figure 3.1 The Process of a Typical Science Talk—*"How Did Rice Plants Begin?"*

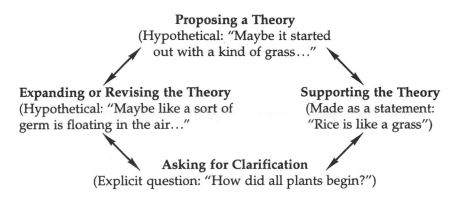

Proposing a Theory
(Hypothetical: "Maybe it started
out with a kind of grass..."

Expanding or Revising the Theory
(Hypothetical: "Maybe like a sort of
germ is floating in the air..."

Supporting the Theory
(Made as a statement:
"Rice is like a grass")

Asking for Clarification
(Explicit question: "How did all plants begin?")

Molly's analogy, "like humans started out as animals." And requests for clarification are often asked as specific questions directed at a particular speaker and a particular statement. The children are usually very clear about which idea they don't understand, and who said it.

Further, from my experience in these talks, it is very rare that a theory is rejected out of hand. The children generally work quite hard to use an idea. For example, in this talk, there was a section when John attempted to build an idea based on the notion that people might have evolved as a result of what they ate: "But the apes might have changed with the different things they ate." The children attempted to work with that idea, even though they weren't able to accept John's use of the word "ate" as applicable to plants.

SHELLY: Like rice couldn't eat something. It could have a lot of water. Rice could have water. They don't eat dirt.
ANDY: Plants will eat anything that's a chemical.
MOLLY: Some plants sort of do eat, like, they need the sunshine, sort of like humans used to eat, and they need water.

And later:

PAUL: If what the apes ate make them turn into humans, then you'd think that would happen the same thing with plants. Maybe a special kind of water.
JOHN: Probably... like salt water.

John's idea, although it was later dropped, was never swiftly rejected. As Science Talks progress, almost every idea is taken seriously and worked with for a time. The children know what Bakhtin has pointed out: Language is socially constructed, and new ideas emerge from the meeting and blending of voices.

Finally, there is a point in almost every talk when the children make a leap in their thinking that in some way reconciles the creative and imaginative exercise of thinking about areas that are completely unknown, with the application of recently acquired prior knowledge. The disruption and confusion of voices and the disorder that signals that achievement occur when the children realize that a piece of knowledge they have about science in the present, or the known, has an application that helps them construct a bridge to the unknown. It is the point at which critical and creative thinking deeply mesh to produce a dialogic outcome that pushes their boundaries out from a knowledge of the particular (flowers require pollination to produce new seeds), to a deeper understanding of the general (perhaps new seeds such as rice can be produced from cross-pollination of like plants, such as grasses). That outcome is exciting to witness and is often the starting point for further study, either from the realization of a new and more sophisticated question "How did *all* plants begin?" or from the desire to pursue the new synthesis of knowledge and imagination, for example, with a study of pollination.

By examining the development of Science Talks, looking for the logic of both the children's ideas and their talk behaviors, and working to understand the ways in which children co-construct and elaborate upon their own ideas, I am better able to follow the path of their ideas and to witness the points at which their collaboration results in new and more sophisticated understandings. I also am able to stay out of their way, as it were, because I have come to trust that the talks are purposeful and logical and that the children's desire to come to an intelligent answer collaboratively guides them as they attempt to construct theories together. The following chapter will extend this discussion by taking a closer look at theories and how they emerge.

CHAPTER 4

Theory Building as an Irrational Activity

Science progresses only through bold theories. (Al Linn, Seismologist, 1993)

It is precisely because the drive toward discovery is in a sense irrational that is it so powerful. (Holton, 1973, p. 390)

Scientific theories begin as imaginative constructions. They begin, if you like, as stories, and the purpose of the critical or rectifying episode in scientific reasoning is precisely to find out whether or not these stories are about real life. (Medawar, 1982, p. 53)

FRANNY: Well, then, I have an idea because if we went way, way, way back, then, then, we couldn't say that there was no grass and

T: Was there ever a time, you think, when there was no grass?

FRANNY: I know. . . . But then, if there was no grass, there might not be any water, so of course plants couldn't grow. There might not be any water if, because the plants need water to grow.

SHELLY: Franny you're, right! So it coulda been that it's too hot. That water started nature!

T2: Water that started nature?

SHELLY: You know

DONALD: There couldn't because

SHELLY: because

T: Wait, wait, wait, wait, wait, wait, wait, wait, wait! I'm getting confused.

FRANNY: Like we can't grow without water, and

SARAH: We can't live without water.

SHELLY: Plants can't live without water.

ANDY: I can't live without it!

DONALD: Monkeys, monkeys can't live without water!

> Excerpt from the Science Talk,
> *"How did nature begin?"* —Grades 1 and 2

In my experience the emergence of a new theory during a Science Talk is, as I pointed out in Chapter 3, always accompanied by an uproar and a temporary dissolution of order in the group. Even teachers tend to fall apart temporarily, either out of excitement, confusion, or sheer astonishment at the power of the children to generate a bold, new idea. This confusion is furthered by the fact that the theory is often crystallized in a matter of seconds, and, most especially for adult listeners, it seems to appear out of the blue. In actual fact, as I attempted to show in Chapter 3, a new theory emerges slowly and carefully, and represents a synthesis of the different tangents the children have discussed.

Yet the overall effect of a new idea is that it causes a temporary breakdown of order. And after watching and wondering about that breakdown, after experiencing it myself, after listening to it on tape and noticing that it is accompanied by shouts, squeals of excitement, and several breakaway conversations (these usually are all indicated by the words "disturbance" on a transcript, if someone else is transcribing my tape), I have begun to think about what, exactly, theorizing is. What does the process of theory making entail? Is it a "rational" activity, or is it a kind of thinking that defies neat characterization?

THE ROLE OF THEORY IN SCIENCE

In order to say we have developed a knowledge of science, we must be able to say we have an understanding of the function, structure, and generation of scientific theories. (Duschl, 1990, p. 96)

Duschl, in arguing for a new conceptualization of science education, proposes that to be scientifically literate, students of science must understand how "scientific knowledge is constructed and reconstructed" (p. 40). Like Lemke (1990), who deplores the presentation of science in schools as a series of "truths" that deny the constantly shifting understanding of the world that science presents, Duschl (1990) points out the dangers of "final form presentations of science" (p. 68).

In my opinion, both scholars are proposing that students enter as fully as possible into the kind of thinking and action that real science engages. Yet when we begin to examine what kind of world the scientist lives in, we find that it is not simply a rational world where theories are calmly proposed and carefully argued. Descriptions of the work of research scientists (Holton, 1978; Latour, 1987; Latour & Woolgar, 1979;

Lynch, 1985; Medawar, 1982; Watson, 1968) allow us to enter a world where dialogue among colleagues is critical to the generation and development of theories; where creative processes that one might delegate to the artist or poet, such as intuition, imagination, visualization, and wonder, work hand in hand with experimentation (Cobb, 1994; Holton, 1973; Medawar, 1982; Rothenberg, 1979); where emotion, morality, and religion inform and motivate the scientist (Gould, 1989; Holton, 1978); and where the act of writing and communicating the final outcomes of research erases the private process of science (Holton, 1973; Medawar, 1982).

In the end, of course, the theories that are presented to the world are rational and orderly, but the process of generating ideas and developing and changing theories is, in itself, complex and often disorderly. Contrary to what some philosophers would have us believe, humans are not rational beings. They can be rational, but their best thinking does not spring from rationality.

THE RELATIONSHIP BETWEEN THEORY AND COMMUNITY

Familiarity has a cognitive underpinning. (Ochs & Taylor, 1992)

It is also clear from many of those accounts that theories are often the result of collaborations among scientists and that in many cases they are co-constructed. In this collaborative process, ideas are challenged, abandoned, refined, and transformed through collegiality. This is the kind of work that I see children doing in Science Talks. When given the forum, they naturally engage in theoretical speculation about a question. The speculation is usually couched in the "maybe that" mode, as we have seen in Chapter 3, but that mode is unusually flexible and open ended, filled with metaphor, analogy, imagination, and wonder (Gallas, 1994), and the children use it as a community engaged in *dialogue* about science.

I would maintain that for most children and adult students of science, the motivation to theorize is closely associated with trust in the intentions of the community in which it occurs. Because theories and new ideas generally are proposed through talk, and in a public forum, the notion of safety, or "familiarity," and its association with the acquisition of the discourse of science must be considered.

As Ochs and Taylor (1992) point out, friends, family members, and colleagues can challenge and transform a story, or an account of an event, without dissolving a relationship. The same process must happen in a classroom for a teacher and children to achieve new levels of synthesis and understanding when studying any subject. Saying what you think about a question on which you are not an expert is extremely risky. To be fully engaged, the student must trust that the ideas put forth will not be treated perjoratively and will be worked with as part of the classroom dialogue.

Science Talks, which occur regularly and over a long period of time, have the potential to help all children think out loud about a difficult question or problem without fear of being wrong. Children say what they think, revealing naive and magical theories that they normally would keep to themselves. Thinking out loud, and the degree of trust it implies in the intentions of the group, are critical to raising the voices of less verbal children. In a classroom where there are no opportunities to talk together without teacher monitoring of the talk, children will not reveal these incorrect, but closely held, beliefs. Thus, as a teacher, I cannot engage all of my students in the study of science unless a critical level of familiarity and collegial talk is achieved. *Real collaboration results in a process of decentering on the part of the child and, hence, cognitive growth!*

THE INFRASTRUCTURE OF THEORIES

We are dealing here not with resolvable puzzles, but with the raw material of the scientific (and not only the scientific) imagination. (Holton, 1978, p. 20)

In considering the kinds of theories that young children propose and develop in Science Talks, it is helpful to work again with the concepts of "thematics" (Holton, 1978) and "epistemic self-portraits" (Toulmin, 1972; see Chapters 1 and 2), and to view children's theories as emanating from within the domain of the creative imagination. Further, the idea that children's thinking can be viewed as a sort of "conceptual ecology" (Posner, Strike, Hewson, & Gertzog, 1982) offers a way for teachers to understand the components of children's theories. Within the framework of conceptual ecology, students' theories are viewed as constructed from different features: anomalies, analogies and metaphors, epistemological commitments, metaphysical beliefs and concepts, and other kinds of knowledge (observed, written, recounted). Adapting these ideas about the underpinnings of theory to children's thinking explicates both the cognitive, creative, and psychic sources of their theories, and the foundations of both their questions and their misconceptions.

Epistemological Commitments

Within the context of Science Talks, children regularly make reference to the features described above. There are always comments and brief discussions of epistemological positions when children state their beliefs about where authoritative knowledge resides.

Tony: (in response to another child's reference to a book he owned) But wait, but what if they, like, answer what *they* think . . . but other people think other things. Like what if I said to Danny, "You have to read this book," or something and he says, "No." That would be right because he has a different mind of which book he wants to read, and everything, and it's the same thing as how the earth got made. . . because people think different things. The book might try to give you an idea, and other people might be trying to give you another idea.
Excerpt from the Science Talk, *"How do leaves change color?"*—Grade 1

Children do not naturally view science as infallible. Not only do they reject the primacy of books, but they also question the scientist's final word on a subject: "Just because a scientist says it's so doesn't mean it is. Because how do they know everything that ever happened?" Further, many children believe that a single explanation for an event is simplistic: "It doesn't have to be just one idea, because how can we say only one thing happened. It could be many different things."

For example, in a Science Talk titled, "How did the dinosaurs die?" to which they brought considerable knowledge, the children cited several possible theories, some of which emanated purely from the discussion: meteorites hit the earth; volcanoes erupted and poisoned the air; plants died because of bad weather, and then the plant eaters died, followed by the meat eaters; too many dinosaurs populated different areas and food ran out; a disease might have attacked a particular group and then spread as the animals moved about. These children were clear about how knowledge of this subject was obtained: People should study the places where bones were found, and "you could study the bones and see if they had the right food, or if there was too much heat."

Metaphysical Positions

Science Talks also reveal children's early notions of metaphysics. Some children will initially cite God as a causal factor in relation to any question, but when I explain to them that their belief in God stops us from having a discussion and is also something *I* cannot discuss in school (due to laws separating church and state), they very respectfully put that solution to all questions aside, and join in the talks. From that point we can begin to see what other kinds of metaphysical beliefs operate in the talks. Some children, usually girls, will cite "mother nature" as the locus of order in the universe. Often, this belief is voiced early on and then is retired as the child becomes more involved in the talks.

More experienced talkers, however, often spend time clarifying large concepts such as "life," "beginning," or "matter" before a science talk can get underway. For example, before answering the question, "Does the universe end?" the word *universe* must be defined.

"The universe is, like, what people think . . . because you've got
     to know what 'the universe' means to answer that question."
"The universe is everything that can be thought or that is here
     right now."
"The universe is space . . . like, I'm not the universe, this table
     isn't the universe, it's out *in* the universe."
"There might not be only one universe, there might be a couple."

Uses of Analogy and Metaphor

As the discussions progress, many theories are proposed in the form of analogies or metaphors. The children's fluid use of these devices enables them to describe very difficult ideas through images and references to seemingly unrelated sources. For example, when trying to propose a theory about why the earth turned, Michael said, "The earth, sun, and moon are kind of like magnetic marbles." He was not able to say any more than that, but clearly he was beginning to approach a theory from a compelling image. It is often the use of metaphor and analogy that confounds adult listeners and leads them to discount children's statements as misconceived or naive. However, as later chapters will show, these creative devices often push the children's thinking to new levels of sophistication and reasoning. (For a more detailed analysis of metaphor and analogy in Science Talks, see Gallas, 1994, Chapter 7.)

General Knowledge

Finally, the children use a vast array of knowledge from other areas to form their arguments. They cite their acute observations of the natural world, facts they've learned in nonfiction books, stories adults have told them, fiction they've read, movies, television shows, and their own true to life adventures with particular phenomena, such as electricity. Sometimes, when a question is too confounding and abstract, these sources form the basis of the entire Science Talk. It's as if, by citing these sources, the children can begin to define the boundaries of a subject. One might look at the process as a method for beginning to approach the development of a theory, similar to the model described by Duschl (1990), in which the scientist collects data, looks for patterns, and begins to develop theories to explain those patterns. The following chapter will illustrate how the process of theory development in the early stages of answering a question emerges naturally, but painfully, from collaborative discussions.

CHAPTER 5

When the Question Is Too Hard

Encountering a question that is too difficult is a much rarer occurrence than might be imagined. When it happens, however, it provides an unusual opportunity to see how children go about trying to tackle a tremendously difficult question. In effect, I can observe the early stages of the process of developing a scientific theory: The children collect data from their lives and then make attempts to find some patterns. In these cases, the first Science Talk will be primarily a time when children muster their collective knowledge about a phenomenon, knowledge that, as I said in Chapter 4, emanates from many areas of experience. For the purposes of illustrating how this kind of knowledge is identified and worked with by a group of children, I will use a Science Talk titled, "What makes electricity?" which took place in a third grade classroom.

WHAT MAKES ELECTRICITY?

Initially, several children proposed their most immediate experiences with what they knew to be signs or sources of electricity.

JOHN: Electricity is kind of like, I think it's kind of like lightning.

ALEX: Yeah. Electricity maybe is

JOHN: It's static, too.

AMY: It's static, like when you rub against something, you know. Like when you rub against a balloon and you stick up.

JOHN: Or it can be fire 'cause, um, um, um, when, um, lightning hits, um, something, sometimes it can catch on fire.

ALEX: Like, um, like, like you ca-, like water makes electricity sometimes.

The discussion continued with other children citing evidence of their experiences with static electricity, and then Susan introduced her understanding of Ben Franklin's experiences with electricity.

SUSAN: The reason, how I think electricity started is because maybe like, maybe something happened to some of the acids in the earth or something, and it just and it just went into the air when it rained and it just came down and it started an electricity storm and then, and then like, in the Middle Ages when Ben Franklin was around, um, he realized that lightning was electricity and, and like, and like, other people didn't really know that lightning was electricity and somewhere around the core of the earth the electricity started, or something.

In this case, Susan was citing vague historical evidence that she could recall and was pairing it with equally vague references to "acids" and "the core of the earth."

The other children had difficulty with her statement, most probably because of her intermingling of scientific terms with evidence from a story that they also had heard about Ben Franklin. They asked Susan a series of questions: "What did you say about the, um, about the electricity coming down with the rain?"; "You said lightning was electricity but it stored it, in the earth or something?"; "How could lightning be stored in, like, some kind of rock or mineral?" but were unable to gain more clarity about her ideas. John returned to his association of fire with electricity.

JOHN: Why is fire kind of like electricity, 'cause every time lightning hits something, it starts on fire. It doesn't always start fire, but . . . you know how you make fire? You can, um, that's probably like some, like electricity. They probably use elec-, they probably use fire, or when the lightning, when it's lightning or something. I don't know how to . . . They could just start a fire, and probably put some, um, put some wires over it, probably hook, hook it up to something, and plug it in, probably, probably it might work.

John was groping around, culling his knowledge of fire, and of electricity being associated with wires that were "hooked up." His halting speech shows that he is not clear but is reaching into his memory and attempting to make associations between different kinds of knowledge.

A bit later, Susan makes a connection to John's use of the hooked up metaphor, and her own earlier attempt to cite Ben Franklin's experiments. Her reference point, however, is a well known children's story that had been made into a movie.

SUSAN: This is sort of related to Benjamin Franklin except this is in a movie, it's called "City Mouse and Country Mouse." And when city mouse, actually, country mouse comes to see . . . city mouse comes to see country mouse and country mouse doesn't like his brother anymore 'cause he's like, "Oh, this bed is too country like," and so he runs out, the country mouse runs out into a lightning storm and he keeps getting hit, and when he gets hit, the lightning—his tail fizzes, sort of like, electricity is going in.

At this point, Joanne makes an attempt to summarize what the children had been talking about and, perceiving correctly that most children associated lightning with electricity, poses a question that later led to a subsequent Science Talk.

JOANNE: I kind of agree with lots of people because I don't know what might have happened, but, like what Susan said, that, that under the ground there might be something under that or something. There might be something under the ground that we don't know about and it could be like everyone else said, because, there might be different ways to make lightning, but I mean like, maybe there's all different ways probably, but the only thing that . . . it's almost like, it's almost like, everybody's talking about lightning, but how did we get lightning then? How did we know that lightning is there?
CHLOE: That's sort of like, leading on to another question. How is lightning made?

A bit later, Gabrielle introduces a new idea using the mixing of acids as a source of electricity: "Two acids mixed together and then they keep growing and growing until they form lightning and then it comes down as electricity." This begins a new phase when children add more anecdotes of their personal associations with the topic of electricity, for example, the following:

BERNICE: . . . you can do this with a wool hat or something. You rub your head with a wool hat and then, or you can rub it with a balloon and your hair sticks up. And the second thing is that I have seen like, this thing that, it's near where my mom goes shopping in Filene's Basement . . . It's so high everything can crash into it, and, like, it's something with electricity . . .

APAR: In a book once, I heard that electricity was studied by the ancient Greeks . . .

SUSAN: Well, in this book, there was this book about Zeus . . . and there was this lightning god . . .

JOANNE: Well, in this book it had, it has, it has questions, and then it answers them for you . . . But it talked about electricity and it said electricity was made from lightning . . .

APAR: Well, um, electricity, you put two wires together, black and red and that's how you get electricity and you might even get electrocuted.

PAO: Well . . . you know how you are vacuuming, you know those little plugs you stick the wire into? And those little things sticking up . . . Well one time the vacuum cleaner was running and my brother pulled the wire out and I saw these little sparks. What I think was, the electricity that goes in the wire travels in little thin lines like string and it goes into the wire.

JOHN: . . . I think it was once, one time my brother stuck a spoon in a socket . . . Um, I put a spoon in the socket . . . There were these sparks . . . And, um, sometimes when we have blackouts, I think this might be true, but what I said, probably they follow lightning . . .

John's introduction of the term "blackouts" causes Chloe to see a conflict within the general association of lightning as the source of electricity.

CHLOE: Oh, well, as everybody said, electricity comes from lightning, usually there's an electric building where they make everything work and everything, and . . . I know that, so if it is lightning that causes that then why, when lightning hits that stuff, well all the electric stuff, and stuff, that's when we have blackouts . . . Because electricity, electricity comes from lightning. Then why, when lightning hit the building where most people's electricity comes from, do we have blackouts?

Chloe's question is followed by more examples of electricity that are not so closely aligned with lightning: exploding vacuum cleaners, falling telephone wires, electricity poles, sparking plugs, power houses, forks melting in electrical outlets, and microwave ovens. As the talk ended, these examples were told as stories of the children's encounters with the technology associated with electricity, but the children had not ventured to propose any particular theories that answered the question.

FINDING PATTERNS

What they had been able to do in the talk was to take a survey of their knowledge about electricity in the world. In effect, they had clearly identified that they knew which natural and man-made phenomena were associated with electricity: lightning, static electricity, batteries, plugs, power plants, electrical towers, appliances, and so forth. As their teacher, Dianne Litts, and I observed this and then pondered what to do to help them go further with their thinking, this information enabled us to plan what might come next. We decided to have a follow-up discussion about lightning, focused on Joanne's and Chloe's question. That Science Talk, however, was even more diffuse than the first. Essentially the children could not move beyond talking about the fact that lightning occurred, and they knew it was associated with electricity. That discussion digressed to more stories, but the character of these was one of personification and mythology; for example:

ALEX: Maybe the clouds get really . . . this is what I used to think. I thought they got really, really mad, and their heads started to heat up so they . . . that's how thunder was 'cause he started yelling at someone, like, "Aaaghh!" And then, so all of this hot stuff came from his head so it went . . . then I got scared of it 'cause I thought it would hurt your head . . . I thought when you get hit by lightning, sparks would come out of your head. And when it was raining, I always put this big, like a towel and I had a big sweatshirt . . .

Clearly, this question also was much too difficult for the children to work with. Even their very rich experience with the evidence of electricity did not enable them to find any patterns that might lead to conceptual explanations for the origins of electricity.

WORKING WITH PRIOR KNOWLEDGE

At that point, Dianne decided to take what the children knew and work with it in an attempt to explain how electricity is made. She constructed a lesson, which I observed, using direct instruction, creative movement, reference to textbooks, and demonstrations. The lesson lasted for more than 40 minutes, and the children were extremely attentive. Their work on electricity continued throughout the week. Two weeks later we had another Science Talk to assess the effect of the formal lesson. This discussion was much more technical than the first and used the new idea of electrons as a reference point.

ALY: Like we talked about the electrons rubbing together and making static electricity. And um, and a cloud filled with water has a different amount of electrons than a cloud filled with not much water. And when they rub together, that makes static electricity and lightning.

JOHN: Everything is matter and if something moves against another thing, the electrons from the different atoms try to, um, get back to the original place, and it creates static electricity, like in your hair.

SALLY: In order for static electricity to work, we need, you would need to rub atoms together, wouldn't you?

BETH: Yeah.

SALLY: So then, so then, electricity from the battery has to be, there has to be something inside that to be rubbing against atoms.

BETH: Probably, part of it is lead.

SALLY: Yeah, there is lead.

?: And some acid.

CHLOE: How do you know there was lead?

SALLY: Because at my old school we split a battery, and like, it was hard to split cause we had to use, like, this machine to split it, and there was, like, that thick lead around the inner side to protect it.

ALLEN: And also, they can't put, like, plastic in these or something. Then the electrons can't travel through the plastic very good. The atoms, the plastic, um, they, um hold on to the electrons more than the metal does.

CHLOE: Also, if there was plastic inside a battery, it would melt.

In the discussion, the children spoke about the movement of electrons and exchanges of energy. They used their new knowledge to discuss the same phenomena they had cited in their earlier talks as evidence of electricity, such as lightning, electrical fires, and fuse boxes, but this time they explained how those phenomena worked.

Sometimes, in order for children and their teachers to move toward the construction of theories, they must begin with the most basic and limited knowledge and move slowly toward explanations. Although the first Science Talk on electricity had resulted only in the development of a series of references to the topic, it enabled Dianne and me to see that even though the question was much too hard for the children, there was some material for us to work with, including their fascination with the topic.

It is interesting to note that prior to these talks many of these children had had experiences with "Battery and Bulb" units, in which they used batteries and wires to make circuits that lit the bulbs. Clearly, however, these kinds of exploratory experiences with the *results* of electricity did not begin to help them approach their question about the origins of electricity. That question is one that also has been asked by both first and second graders in my classroom. Many children are fascinated with the phenomenon of electricity in their daily lives and want to understand it on some level. Hence the question.

Yet for all practical purposes, for children the study of electricity is one of the first instances when science moves from the concrete to the completely abstract. Very few adults can correctly and clearly explain what makes electricity. It is something that needs to be explored and talked about again and again. In the case of this third grade class, only after the early talks and instruction in a more formal context, were they able to sort out the meaning of their previous experiences with batteries and bulbs, and some of their observations of static electricity and lightning.

As I pointed out in the Introduction, and as Chapter 6 will show, often the lessons we provide for children for the purpose of expanding their understanding of important concepts, fall short of our teaching goals because we have not directly identified, and discussed, the seminal question that forms the underpinning of our intentions in presenting the materials. *Inquiry alone does not suffice.* Children can construct rich meanings when presented with rich materials, but the meanings they construct, without reflection and discussion, are often diffuse, mysterious, and laden with misconceptions.

CHAPTER 6

Misconceptions as a Search for Origins

After a few years of documenting Science Talks, my work expanded to include children I formerly had taught in first grade. At that point I had the uncomfortable experience of witnessing talks about subjects that I thought I had taught well. The more I expanded my research community, the more frequent the occurrence. At first I was surprised and, in the tradition of my graduate training, which emphasized developmental teaching, I attributed the children's incorrect theories to their lack of readiness for the topic I had presented. In other words, when I taught the unit on "Sun, Moon, Seasons, and Shadows," some children were simply not developmentally ready to absorb the information, even though I had painstakingly provided a wide array of demonstrations and hands-on activities.

Gradually, however, I realized that my former students were voicing their misconceptions when they encountered, after the fact, questions that went to the heart of the units I had taught, what I now call the Original Question. Although I had thoroughly and conscientiously taught a unit in science, I had neglected to ask the most important question prior to teaching the unit, the question that lay beneath the surface of the unit's goals and activities. Often the same children who might have participated in a unit on plants, or the moon, or "Sink and Float," or "Batteries and Bulbs" would, in the following year or two, ask the seminal question: "How did plants begin?"; "How did the moon begin?"; "Where did the water come from?"; "What makes electricity?"; "Why do seasons change?"; "How did nature begin?" Then, as they discussed the question, I would witness the misconceived fruits of my teaching.

SOLICITING KNOWLEDGE AS OPPOSED TO THEORY

In essence, the dialogue about a subject had not been formally initiated, and I had not seen the children's "theoretical map" of the subject we were going to study. Even though in the tradition of conscientious teaching I would identify the children's basic knowledge and questions before the unit started, through the use of charts titled, "What I Know," "What I Think I Know," and "What I Want to Know," I would get only a partial sense of the degree of information or misinformation they had. Somehow these kinds of assessment tools missed both the most important questions and the more deeply rooted "naive theories," or misconceptions, that the children held on to throughout the course of instruction.

Although there are many ways to assess children's prior knowledge about a subject, in my opinion the nature of misconceptions is that they reside in a different place than basic knowledge and observation. Just as I proposed that the source of theorizing is located in an irrational, or nonrational place, I would propose that misconceptions do not live in the mind in the same place as basic knowledge, although they are certainly developed in association with that knowledge. Because misconceptions are in fact theories, they too live within the domain of "conceptual ecology" (see Chapter 4). As a result they are not easily elicited, because generally they are the silent, contemplative, and carefully guarded stories that children construct about their world, *and their structure is extremely complex.*

IDENTIFYING THE SEMINAL QUESTION

When I ask children for their knowledge of a subject, they very properly provide whatever *information* they have, as we have seen in Chapter 5. They know, I think, that I am not seeking what they've imagined about lightning or wind, the stars or the moon. Rather, I am asking them to be factual, and they recognize that discourse. Further, when I solicit general questions about plants, for example, children usually respond with information-oriented questions: How long can plants live?; Do all plants need water?; Can plants live without water?; How does a seed grow into a plant?; Why are leaves green? and so on. In the past, before I initiated Science Talks, any questions that weren't of that nature were pushed aside. If a child asked, "Where did the plants come from?" I would avoid that question, feeling that it was impossible to even broach with young children.

I now believe that instruction on a concept or a topic should not commence before the seminal question is asked, and, further, I have found that it takes considerable thought and clarity on the part of teachers to identify what that question might be (although often children spontaneously identify those questions). Even the goals and objectives of a unit of study, although seeming to be stated in terms of conceptual results, do not provide information about what the original question ought to be. I was able to begin thinking about this only because the children I taught would identify the question a year or two later. Clearly, they were still wondering about it in spite of what they had experienced in their studies.

SEARCHING FOR ORIGINS AND SEMINAL THEORIES

When children do identify these questions, the questions reach for superlatives; they search for beginnings and first causes (see Appendix A). And when they attempt to talk about these questions, they struggle to find terms that might explain *many* things. When considering these overarching terms, we can return again to Holton's description of how thematics work in science (see Chapters 1 and 2).

Children speak of "particles," "chemicals," "acids," and "germs," and apply them across many topics, as the talks in this book show. In using these terms, it is clear that the children have heard them used by adults and are attempting to sound scientific. But in looking at the semantic, rather than the social, use of the terms, we can view their application as also reflecting a child's desire to find organizing concepts or patterns that explain, in a unified way, diverse natural phenomena. Often, as Holton points out, these concepts, or themata, persist into adulthood and have a pervasive influence on a individual's understanding (or misunderstanding) of many different subjects. (See Chapter 9 for more discussion of these terms.)

Taken from this vantage point, then, it is important for teachers to ask the deep question (if the children have not). By doing so, we can openly solicit deeply held beliefs, identifying as we do both their complexity and their sources. In this sense, as children talk together, we can discover the map of their theories and use it to construct our teaching, at the same time helping them to "restructure" (Carey, 1986) that map. To illustrate the kinds of theories we might discover, if this process were to precede a unit of instruction, I will describe a Science Talk on the question, "How did the moon begin?" that took place with a class of first and second graders *a full year* after I had taught a lengthy unit on the sun and the moon.

How Did the Moon Begin?

It is interesting to note that this question was asked by a second grader who had participated in our study of the sun and moon. When she asked the question, I made the assumption that, although this was a difficult question that was not dealt with in the moon unit, it had been touched upon frequently in another study on the earth that integrated science and geography. That study included discussion and research on the beginnings of our planet and solar system.

I was, however, completely unprepared for the text that emerged as the children struggled to construct a coherent theory. What was most amazing, beyond the spectacular theories that some children held about the origin of the moon, was that after a unit of instruction that included research, moon watching, shadow work, and discussions and demonstrations of the movement of the earth and moon, my second graders had very little basic knowledge to apply to the question. In other words, the unit as I had conceived it, left them with very little useful information.

This talk opened with a statement by Holly, the second grader who had asked the question, that I found almost completely unbelievable. And to make matters worse, the response of the other children showed me that they also had very primitive theories. Even Donald, whom I spoke about in Chapter 2, had difficulty mustering any information to relate to the question.

HOLLY: I think that the moon is made because there's like a lot of stars put together. Like during the day sometimes the moon's not out because the stars come away from the moon, or something, and, and at night when it gets a little darker, it turns into a moon, and, and then some stars go like, if there was a half a moon, like, and then, there's a whole moon, and then, some stars would go away and stay out out so, it could be, so some people could see the stars.

SHELLY: I think maybe, this is partly what I think, that um, I think partly some of it is some rock, like formed as a, a big circle out of the moon you know, so, maybe . . . Like the shine like can be made from stars.

T: You agree to that part of Holly's, but you think it might have something to do with rock?

DONALD: I think maybe it's like, uh, it's like some kind of planet, planet or something, or star or something. Um, exploded or something, and like a white dwarf.

AMY: I think the moon got made by many little, sticky, like stuff that's called particles . . .

?: Yeah.

AMY: that are stuck together. I think they were very sticky, and then they stuck together, and then just, they formed into a circle. . . .

Tom: I think that stars are shiny white things.

Brandy: I think that, um, a, a long time ago, there was a rock, and something like, maybe something from outer space, the air or something, came down and pulled it out, and the stars got mixed in with it you know, and it was like rocky, and the stars got mixed in with it you know and it made circle shapes.

T: made kind of circle shapes, do you want to speak, speak up to everybody . . .

Andy: I think there's this rock before people were made and it started bursting open, and it got so shiny, and I think that we called it the moon.

With the exception of Amy, every child who spoke in this first excerpt was a second grader, and as the talk continued, the children characteristically tried to work with everyone's ideas, but they were not able to come to any closure on the question. For example, Holly went on to modify her first thought by combining it with Amy, Andy, and Shelly's ideas.

Holly: I think that, that a lot of wet crystals, 'cause there was a big huge huge rock, and it blew up and a lot of crystals came out of it and then crystals turned into the moon. And, and then it like, and, it would change, and it would, like, take off half the crystals a day, and I think the stars were made out of crystals.

As the text shows, the children simply could not work effectively with what little information they had. Even Donald, our science buff, worked very hard throughout this talk, but was not able to develop a coherent idea in spite of his large factual knowledge about space.

A few weeks later, as I witnessed a Science Talk in a third grade on the question, "How did plants begin?" and then watched a talk on the same question with my first and second graders, I saw a new twist on the issue of the results of my prior teaching. In this case, neither the second nor the third graders, *all* of whom had participated in extensive plant studies either in my classroom or in other classrooms in the school, were able to approach the question without basing their theories on a "seed" theory.

How Did Plants Begin?

Both classes had generated the question independently, and their discussions essentially correctly revoiced what they had been taught. In fact, in the discussion in the first and second grade, Donald did propose early on an alternative to the seed theory, but he was generally ignored.

SHELLY: When the ground began like, probably there were some
    seeds that were made up in the ground with other stuff, and
    then the seeds grew into plants.
HOLLY: Um, I think that like, I sort of agree with Shelly, when the wa-
    ter comes up, when the water, when it rains, the plants grow.
DONALD: Ferns, ferns were the first plants on earth, and when ferns
    grow up they don't have seeds, so that would mean that . . .
SHELLY: But some plants do come from seeds.
T: Donald said ferns were the first plants on earth. He's saying when
    ferns grow, they don't have seeds. They don't grow from seeds.
DONALD: 'Cause I have ferns in my driveway.

Essentially, Donald's proposition was dropped at that point and never resurfaced, until he tried unsuccessfully one more time to reconcile it with the direction of the discussion: "Maybe ferns evolved into other plants with fruits, and fruits made seeds, and the, the fruits fell off and the seeds went into the ground, and made more plants."

In later parts of the talk, all the children correctly restated knowledge they had acquired in our study of plants, knowledge that had been reinforced by their own observations, their experiments with seeds, books, demonstrations, and home experiences, as illustrated in the following excerpts:

HOLLY: like maybe dogs came and, maybe dogs carry them. I think
    that dogs carry them around 'cause I heard on the radio, like, an-
    imals have seeds on them.
IAN: I think there were like, little particles, sort of in the, maybe like
    in the rocks. They formed together and, um, so, the particles
    they turned into seeds and then they grew, and then they got
    more seeds to make more plants.
MOLLY: I think that, um, dirt and rocks, I think that rocks broke and
    then mixed into, um, dirt, to make seeds.
    (and later)
    Um, there's probably dirt, water, and sun. And it goes together
    probably, um, makes seeds.

In reflecting on this talk, I concluded that the children, with the exception of Donald, simply were unable to contradict the overwhelming evidence that they had observed and been taught, that all plants begin as seeds. What I saw was that, even though we had had experiences with growing plants from cuttings, bulbs, and tubers, that misconception was fiercely guarded precisely because I overlooked this most basic question. Thus, in spite of providing a rich variety of experiences, I had unintentionally contributed to the maintenance of a misconception.

Teachers all over the county teach units on seeds and plants, and carefully foster experimentation, observation, and rich experiences. To be precise, what I found out was but one example of how we must rethink our teaching of science units. In my unit on plants, I obviously focused too heavily on seeds and their life cycles, leading children to believe that that is where all plants come from. In the Science Talk, I witnessed the authority with which my students spoke about plants, seeds, and what they needed to grow, and I realized that even my avid interest and teaching had narrowed their concepts. I had not provided a place for their interest in the origins of things, or the seminal question, primarily because I had never thought about the place of such a question in that kind of study.

RE-EXAMINING OUR STARTING POINTS

As Chapter 5 showed, students who participated in "Battery and Bulb" units also had not had a chance to begin with their question, and I must admit that when I've worked with that unit, the outcome has been the same. Somehow in the process of the study, in spite of all the discussions of circuits, energy, bulbs, and batteries, *electricity* was never really discussed. What makes electricity? Obviously batteries do! I have witnessed talks where fifth grade students who studied optics for several weeks asked, at the end of the unit, "How do mirrors work?" and where young children who had studied seasons throughout the fall and winter, when talking later about the question, "What happens in the winter?" stated that *everything*, including all trees, died each winter. These examples are a few from my limited experience, and I have no doubt that there are hundreds more that I have not come across yet.

What these few instances underscore for me is the care with which teachers and curriculum developers must construct their plans. What is required, I think, is that the adults must reclaim the child's mind and start from the position of desiring to know about beginnings and big ideas. That may guide us in ensuring that our best intentions do not limit, rather than expand, the children's theoretical frameworks.

Science Talk for Synthesis

This chapter will provide a striking contrast to the last. It begins with a question that would not have been conceived of prior to a unit of study, by either the children or myself, and shows how children can use a forum like Science Talks to generate sophisticated questions and synthesize their new knowledge in unexpected and challenging ways.

The question, "Is voice matter?" was asked by a child at the end of a unit on "States of Matter," a required piece of curriculum for the second grade. The unit, primarily for second graders (although first graders participated in almost all activities), was taught by a student teacher, and she followed the curriculum guide very closely, combining demonstrations, experiments, read aloud experiences, and discussions. It was an interesting unit to observe because initially even the question, "What is matter?" resulted in silence and blank stares from the class. The concept of "matter" was completely foreign to the children, but as the unit progressed they were captivated with the idea of identifying different aspects of their world as solids, liquids, and gases, and of relating their basic knowledge of those properties to the experiments and demonstrations.

IS VOICE MATTER?

When Ellen, age 7, asked this question following a demonstration on gases, it seemed to pop out without any context, although the lesson had been focused on how the scent of a perfume moves across a room. I can only conclude that she must have connected the movement of air with the movement of voice. Her question immediately provoked a storm of discussion and argument. She, however, curbed that unorganized discussion by asking if we could have a Science Talk about the question, and that took place the next day.

The talk involved both second and first graders, and immediately focused on defining whether voice takes up space.

Tom: Air takes up, um, space, but does voice?

Lester: I think it sort of does because like, it's like air, and voice is like air so it's

Ellen: Sort of . . .

Tom: Like if you, like if she can blow up a balloon up with your, with your um, with your, um, breath, it, um, must take up, it must be matter, sort of.

Eli: It must be matter sort of, 'cause . . .

Tom: Like if you blow up a balloon, like it takes matter.

Ellen: I think it might be matter because, um, when you talk you breathe out and you breathe in, so . . .

Ellen's premise came to be the central point under dispute in this talk. The children had established a definition of matter early in the talk: Matter takes up space. And because they had established in their study that air, a gas, was matter, and air took up space, then the problematic assertion was that voice always occurred in association with air and, therefore, was matter. Tom began to try to grope around Ellen's argument that voice always had to be associated with air, but he was unclear.

Tom: Yeah, but if you breathe, um, talking, um, you can you still um, when some people talk, um, they're like talking a lot, they have to like, get their breath.

So he tried a different tack.

Tom: If voice is, um, matter, um, is, like, would we be getting squished right now, if it's like, taking up room?

Lester: No, it wouldn't exactly be getting like squished.

Ellen: Because air's taking up space, and it's not squeezing us.

Zach: And it takes up more space than we do.

T: Could you say your question again, Tom?

Zach: How could it not really like

Tom: If, if . . .

Zach: squeeze us

Tom: if voice is matter . . .

Zach: to death?

Tom: why isn't it, like, smushing us against the walls?

Michael: Because air is matter, but when there's like, like take a big wind, for instance. When hurricanes or tornadoes come along, they take up a lot of air, and space, and they are air. But it's just a big quantity of air . . .

Michael had attempted to draw a distinction between wind and air as being different degrees of push, but the relationship to the question of voice "squeezing" was too discreet and the children, at first, couldn't relate to his comparison. A bit later, however, Lester tried to pick up Michael's train of thought.

LESTER: Sometimes the voice waves are, are not as hard as winds can be. Voices waves aren't.

But Ian wanted to return to the original question.

IAN: But how can you tell voice is matter if. . . . It seems like air *doesn't* take up space, but it actually *does*. So, so you can't, you can't exactly tell with air where, like, where it is. There's not like, one piece of air going in a different place. That's not the same as with voice. So, it doesn't seem like it would take up room. It's not like every day you see a chunk of air floating around in the sky.
ELLEN: Not if it's really cold and you're breathing, and it gets really cold.
(Sounds of many children breathing in and out.)
IAN: Yeah, so. You don't see a chunk of voice flying around if someone says something. It's not like you see these words coming up in a chunk of voice flying up into the air. (Pointing into the air) "Ohhhh, there's your voice."

Thus Ian turned the discussion back to the issue of determining whether air and voice were the same. Many of the children were ambivalent, stating at one point that they were the same, and at another that they couldn't be because, as Tom said, "air can't talk." But even that statement was argued.

ELI: Air can sorta talk. Because when, if, if it's blowing really hard you can make a noise.
LESTER: Voice like, like your voice is the sound.

So if even the wind makes a noise, and wind is air, and air is matter, then is noise matter? This led to a further discussion of whether voice and air were inextricably tied.

Iᴀɴ: Um, I want to, um, add something to Ellen's but I'm kind of pro-
testing it. But air, air and voice, I don't think they're the same
thing. 'Cause if, if voice was air, why wouldn't you just be breathing it instead of talking with it, using it to talk.

Mɪᴄʜᴀᴇʟ: We didn't say they were the same, we just said they were
kinda similar.

T: Ian can you ask that question again because some people have,
who've said air is like voice 'cause you breathe out, might want
to respond to that. So Ian, will you ask that again?

Iᴀɴ: Yeah, yeah, I don't, I don't think voice and air would be the
same thing. . . . 'Cause it doesn't seem like they're the same
thing. Voice, you talk with it, and air, you breathe. So, if they
were the same thing, if they were just air, you might not talk
'cause you wouldn't have any voice.

Ian's struggle to draw a line between voice, as a means of communication, and air as separate from that, led to a long exchange on language. At this point, Ian propelled the children to move toward a
definition of voice as language with a function and a purpose: "How
come you talk instead of breathing?" They cited the fact that some
animals couldn't talk, and some humans couldn't either. (Says Ian:
"Yeah, my sister uses sign language.") Voice, the children agreed, was
something associated with talking.

Eʟɪ: For instance, for instance, pretend I was the BFG. [Eli is referring to *The BFG*, a children's book by Roald Dahl that we had
read as a class. The BFG has large, supersensitive ears that can
hear the faintest of sounds.] Pretend I was the BFG, and I see a
ladybug, and everybody thinks the ladybug doesn't talk. Because
of the big ears, um, the BFG can hear that she was talking . . .
The reason why we have our voice is because we can talk but
some animals like the ladybug would think the same thing. They
can't speak everything like we can.

This very different metaphor causes a disturbance. Eli is trying to point
out that voice is voice only if we hear and understand it. It's a matter
of perception. The children find this idea very difficult. They want
voice to mean talk. Eli, working in an extremely analytic mode, pushes
the distinction between voice as sound, and words as different aspects
of speech: one physical, the other learned and cognitive.

Pᴀᴜʟ: Eli, um, you don't, you're not born with your voice, you learn
it . . . from other people.

ELI: Yes, but then you learn words, but then how can you speak? If you're not born with a voice, how do you speak? It's not like you open your mouth, and you say something?

ELLEN: I think that those tubes that make you talk, um, whatever, um, aren't, um, totally developed and you have, and you also have to try to learn to talk also.

Later Eli responds to Ellen.

ELI: But Ellen, what you said *does* make a difference. But, um, you have to learn, *and*, you have to have a voice.

The discussion digressed again to the distinction between air and voice, and the children searched for physical evidence that voice and air were joined.

ZACH: I think voice is matter because like, when you talk, you can feel something like hot on your hand. If you put your hand near you mouth and if you don't talk, you don't have something hot on your hand.

IAN: I just tried that experiment and what I found out, see, I said, "I can." and I found out that when I . . . That hot stuff that I felt on my hand is just breath. I was just breathing.

ELI: But Zach, if that is true, then why can't we really see it happening? Why can't we really see it happening?

MICHAEL: I don't know. It's like air, you can't see air happen.

ZACH: You can see it on frosty days.

MICHAEL: Yeah, you can. You see your breath. And your breath is air.

But Eli and Ian had made a point: If voice is matter, why can't we see it in some form? Finally, as the talk ends, Nate, who has not spoken until this time, makes a statement, bringing the discussion full circle.

NATE: Well, if you didn't have those tubes in your body, you couldn't speak. . . . If you were trying to speak, you would try to speak, you'd say nothing. You were saying air.

So, in a reductionist sense, without effective vocal cords there would be no sound, and in the absence of sound you would have just air.

Did the children ever come to an answer? Not in the formal sense, because there was never consensus. But Nate's final statement in essence summarized Ian's and Eli's points that air and voice are not the same and, therefore, voice is not matter.

HARNESSING THE IMAGINATION FOR SCIENCE

Generating seminal questions and/or synthesizing questions both involve an act of the imagination: The child takes a point of curiosity or wonder and uses it to formulate a question. That act of questioning alone is a remarkable thing! My childhood was one in which I hardly ever dared to ask such a question, and certainly no one solicited them. That was a loss for my entire educational process. When the children I work with begin to ask their questions, whether the questions emerge as a beginning point for a study or as a result of a study, they are emanating from the creative imagination, from a point of wonder.

As this talk shows, however, the synthesizing question, while also asked with imagination, represents a very high level of intellectual activity. It moves us beyond the "maybe that" and "perhaps" mode of talk into one of pure conjecture. Notice in this talk how the tentative phrases discussed in Chapter 3 are absent, and how the children's propositions combine ideas they have taken both from the states of matter unit and from their observations of their physical experience of the world. Notice also that the ideas are heavily interspersed with questions that seek clarity and fine distinctions: "If you're not born with a voice, how do you speak?"; "If voice was air, why wouldn't you just be breathing it instead of talking with it?"

Finally, there is a qualitative difference in the way theories are generated in this talk compared, for example, with the talk, "How Did the Moon Begin?" (see Chapter 6 and Appendix B), even though both kinds of talks serve the children's learning. The moon talk began with a seminal question that had never been identified as a starting point for study, and the content of the children's theories, instead of being based on information and ideas that they had learned about the moon, was grounded in the stories of their imagination. In essence, what I saw was a landscape of their imagination. The question was asked, and then laid out beside it were the rich and creative stories of explanation that each child had so naturally, and naively, constructed.

While I see both questions as acts of the imagination, the second talk was clearly constructed with reference to actual classroom studies and was based on physical data and solid prior concepts. It represents to me a distinct movement into another level of serious scientific discourse, one that cannot be achieved unless children have many opportunities to ask, discuss, study, and then refine their questions to reflect increasingly more complex and sophisticated understandings of their world.

CHAPTER 8

Building Curriculum from Children's Questions

Plasma is like a oracle or a wise man. It remembers everything.
—Ricky, age 8

Many years ago, when I first started teaching young children, I would spend time with each class exploring their ideas about human anatomy. Our explorations often would begin with one child's spontaneous drawing of the human body, shown as an x-ray. Characteristically the drawing would include a heart, a few bones floating around in the arms and legs, and a brain. The obvious absence of information that the drawing would reveal would immediately launch me into a flurry of activity on human anatomy. I would ask all the children to do a similar drawing, and inevitably all the drawings would be equally simple. Then we would spend weeks looking at books and diagrams; taking apart what I used to call "the bionic man," that is, disassembling and reassembling a life-sized model of the human body complete with organs and musculature; sketching; and talking. When we finished, all the children would draw a final picture of the human body, and, of course, their drawings would show a new understanding of some of what was inside the human body. Newly present in the pictures would be the brain, skeleton, stomach, intestines, perhaps even a liver or lungs. This piece of work was a very exciting one for all of us and fueled some of my early thinking about the role of the arts in the classroom.

When I began to work with Science Talks, questions about the human body were less common. As Appendix A shows, most of the children's science talk questions focus on natural phenomena such as weather or on origin questions. Also, as I pointed out earlier, originally I did not use the talks to develop curriculum, preferring to let them be times when children could wonder out loud about the world. Eventually, though, small studies began to emerge (such as the work on electricity described in Chapter 5) from talks that I or another teacher just couldn't ignore, either because of the misconceptions that were being voiced or because the children's questions coincided with a unit of study already being planned.

Three years ago my class of first and second graders began to ask questions about human biology, and those questions continued for well over 12 months. The questions popped up with such frequency that I realized they were not isolated thoughts, but rather were multiplying at an unusual rate and reflected a community of children's mutual interest. They were different from other science talk questions in that, with a few exceptions, they were system-oriented rather than focused on beginnings. Following is a summative list of questions as they were asked:

> How do your bones stay together?
> How do your eyes change shape?
> How do people age?
> How does the brain work?
> What is blood for?
> How does a baby grow inside?
> How do legs work?
> How is blood made?
> Why are veins different colors?
> How do we grow?
> Why, when you pinch yourself, does it hurt?
> How do our dreams get into our head?

DEVELOPING AN INFORMAL CURRICULUM

The curriculum that evolved from these questions is interesting in that it was based almost entirely on the children's continuing desire to know more. With many science talk questions, the children are satisfied simply to talk about the question. They will not ask to know the "real" answer, or worry about whether their answers were correct. Perhaps that is because many of the questions they ask are so complex, and, as they say to each other, "scientists don't even know the real answer for sure." It is the asking and the talking that are the focus of those kinds of talks.

With these questions, however, things were slightly different, and as a result I decided to pursue the answers in an informal way, what one might term an unintrusive strategy. I think that my goal was to help the train of thought on human biology continue, but to stay out of the way of the children's questions and curiosity. Sometimes it seems that when teachers intervene in children's interests, they defuse the children's energy and desire to know, rather than fueling it. Children know when we are "taking over" their agenda. They can sense when the "I wonder" in their questions is absorbed into a teacher's "let's find out and show" agenda.

How Do Our Bones Stay Together?

Thus the first question, "How do our bones stay together?" took shape in response to the children's input. The day after that talk, one child brought in a book on skeletons, which I read at story time. The class had a long discussion on the science talk question, incorporating the information from the book, and came to some closure. I pulled books out of my collection that focused on human and animal skeletons. A week or so later another student brought in a small model of the human skeleton that he and his father had assembled at home, and we kept that in our science center for the rest of the year. Children would go over once or twice a week in pairs and casually examine it and talk about it.

Every now and then a child would bring in a favorite bone from home, and describe it at sharing, telling where he or she had found it and what it was. That, too, would go on the science table. More books arrived. In movement we experimented with the notion of what would happen if we had no bones or if our bones didn't bend. When some children drew in their art journals in the morning, they would do sketches of joints and appendages. The study unfolded in a very leisurely and informal way, and the questions multiplied.

At the same time, it happened that a parent, Michael Rich, of one of the children in my class was a pediatrician. He was very interested in working with the children and came in early in the year, around Halloween, with a skeleton and spoke to the children about the skeletal structure. When the questions began to proliferate, I asked Michael to come in and talk with the children after particular Science Talks. His visits were a high point for all of us. Not only did he bring resources that would have been unavailable to me in the school, but I was able to observe how a practicing scientist worked, *and talked,* with children.

Before Michael came to visit, I would send him pictures the children had drawn directly after their first talk on a question, with their own thoughts about the question written or dictated on the page. I had the children draw for two reasons. The first stemmed from my early work with human anatomy, which I described in the beginning of this chapter: I wanted to have a way to assess what the children knew before we did any work on their question. The second was to give Michael a window into the children's thinking before he came to see us, so that he could see the kinds of theories they had about a system. Following his visit, the children would draw a new picture, again based on the question but with their ideas at that point, and we would continue to build on the question with books and activities.

Beginning with the "Bones" question, it was clear to me that the children saw the functions of the human body in a systemic way. In other words, one function, such as the movement of bones, for example, was inextricably tied to the work of the heart and blood: "Maybe the heart that pumps blood to all the things in the body makes molecules in the bones that stick together, and then it makes the bones."

Whenever we discussed a new question, the heart, blood, and brain were cited as important and connected factors in the functioning of the body. The activity of the blood and heart, especially, were continually discussed as dynamic forces in every question, as in the following statements from two different Science Talks:

> Because your heart controls all your whole body because
> the heart, all the blood and everything, controls it so it's like
> that your heart's the big machine that's controlling your
> body. If you didn't have a heart you wouldn't do what you
> wanted, so the heart, the heart is really the main thing.
> [From *"How do our bones stay together?"*]

> The brain has, well . . . the brain gets blood from the heart
> and the blood makes the heart work I mean the blood
> makes the brain work and the brain directs where you're go-
> ing so that you don't bump into people 'cause if you didn't
> have a brain you wouldn't know where you were going.
> [From *"How does the brain work?"*]

Children postulated that even though messages were formed in the brain, they were carried to all parts of the body by the blood, and the blood acted as a sort of coordinator of the brain's work. Some children went so far as to propose that red and white blood cells were responsible for taking the messages to different parts. White blood cells, for example, would carry a message to the fingers, red somewhere else.

What Is Blood for?

As might be expected from these trends, the talk on the question, "What is blood for?" was very intense. Many children participated, even new English speakers, and bold theories were proposed. Clearly the children had observed their own bodily functions closely, and throughout the prior talks were privately speculating on the function of the blood in their bodies. All of these speculations poured out in this talk, which opened with a cross-reference to our "Brain" talk.

MIKE: I think blood carries like, messages from your body to your legs and arms and head, and from your brain.
MAURICE: You mean your heart.
MIKE: Oh, yeah, from your heart. It brings messages from your brain.
ELLEN: Down to do what? To do what?
MIKE: To do anything. Like I'm talking. The blood is making me talk.
SAM: It is?
MAURICE: The blood helps your tongue, helps *you* talk.

The children seemed happy with this idea, but went on to add other important functions to the work of the blood, almost as if they were summarizing many things they had learned in their casual pursuit of this topic.

AMY: I think that maybe, um, blood brings, like, vitamins and stuff to your body to help it move, and grow, and stuff like that.
SAM: Well, if you didn't have blood what would carry your oxygen around your body so you could live?
CHARLES: You couldn't live.
KELLY: You wouldn't be alive you'd be dead because
SAM: Yeah, because blood carries your oxygen, and it plays an important role for your body because without it you'd probably die.
KELLY: like um, the blood through the tube sends, um, air everywhere and the, and there's like, and, when it comes back there's nothing in it to get more air from you.
SAM: It gets more air from the heart.
KELLY: Yeah.
IAN: And if you didn't have blood all the blood cells that are in there, and all the germs that are in there, all the white blood cells

couldn't eat the germs which would make you sick, which would
eventually make you die.

BILL: You would be dead without your blood anyways.

So blood brought nutrients to the body, helped us move, replenished
oxygen throughout our systems, killed disease, and, as Bill pointed
out, "You would be dead without your blood anyways." These first
and second grade children had an astonishing amount of information
about blood, and they spent the rest of the talk refining these ideas
and constructing new ones. For example, at one point in the talk Noel
introduces a comparison between blood and water:

NOEL: Blood gives us oxygen. It helps us stay alive. Same with, um,
    water in our body. It makes us not just, sort of die.

This thought was built upon a short time later by Sam.

SAM: If blood was just like red water and um, if you got a sickness,
    the sickness wouldn't have, um, the blood in it, wouldn't have
    like, um, like any chance, or whatever, to get the, um, sickness
    away, so you'd get, like, really really sick, if blood was just like
    water rushing through your body.

MAURICE: Yeah, and, and, and blood's thicker, thicker than water.

T: That's a saying, right?

Maurice's free association of blood and water to a saying he'd
heard turned the group's attention to the development of a new metaphor.

RICKY: Like if you have a cut now it doesn't just like, it just comes
    out like, it doesn't come out that much, like, if it was just red wa-
    ter and you got a cut, it, would like, more would come out.

TOM: Yeah, it would start, like, pouring out.

And a bit later:

BILL: And one of the good reasons, one of the good reasons that
    blood is really thick is because, like Ricky was saying, if it were
    red water, I'm just adding on to this in a different way. If there
    were red water, well, blood carries things in it like oxygen and
    proteins and stuff you need. So if it was like, so it's thick, so it
    has more room to carry things that you need to support your

body. So if it were thinner, then it would be so, like, it would be so watery, so it couldn't hold all that, all this stuff in it.

Bill took the notion of thickness of a liquid that Ricky had added, and applied it to a new theory about the density of blood as compared with water and how blood would be able to hold more important "things that you need to support your body." This idea was probably another extension of Bill's understanding of the "States of Matter" unit I discussed in Chapter 7, a unit this class had completed in March, 2 months before this talk on blood.

I thought this was a very difficult idea to follow and wondered at the time who had understood Bill's point. Later in the talk, however, Ian, a first grader, referred to Bill's comment.

IAN: Well I have something sort of adding on to Bill's like if there's water, water can't really even carry a leaf. It can carry a leaf, but it has to have a lot of water like, sort of a little stream, and um, since blood is thicker, it can can hold like, um, blood cells. That's probably about as heavy as leaves.

T: So you're kind of agreeing with Bill that it has more strength and space.

IAN: And you might think that blood cells are always red. They're really not. They're really pinkish, but when it looks all red they look red, but they're actually pinkish. Like probably if you threw a rock into a tub of water it would go down faster than into a tub of blood.

Thus Noel's original comparison of blood and water was developed by the group into a complex metaphor that expanded their original understandings of what blood was for, into a theory about its structure. Some children had certainly made the statement that blood was composed of different kinds of cells and that blood cells carried nutrients and oxygen to the body. Other children had stated that blood traveled through "tubes," helped heal and clean wounds, and protected organs from injury. The new metaphor of blood as "thick" and different from water in structure took all of those pieces of knowledge and placed them into an image that explained how all of those functions could occur. I considered that this had been quite a remarkable collaborative talk that in many ways synthesized much of the earlier work that had gone on informally throughout the year.

As always, right after the talk I asked the children to draw an idea, or ideas, that they felt answered the question best. Their drawings (see, for example, Figure 8.1) summarized the main points of the Science Talk and included the original theory that the blood told the brain what to do. For the next few days, animated conversations about blood continued, and I arranged with Michael to come and speak with us on the question. I sent all the children's drawings home with his child.

EXTENDING THE METAPHORS

Michael arrived in the classroom with books, slides of blood samples, and tubes of blood. As soon as he began to talk with the children about their question, he described the circulatory system as "a highway" and "a river" in the body. He characterized white blood cells as "the soldiers," and blood as "the sap" of our body. Michael personified blood when he spoke about its work in the body: "the blood knows"; he showed a tube of blood that had been centrifuged and described the protein layer as "like cotton candy or angel's hair."

The children immediately began to pepper him with questions about how the blood worked, using personification as easily as he had: "How does the blood know?"; "How do the blood cells get rid of other cells?" Michael answered them in the same terms: "The white blood cells chomp up the old red blood cells, just eat it up like pac man." The questions became more complex and went into new areas. At one point Ricky asked him, referring to the blood cells: "When they're made, do they know what they're s'posed to do, or do they get taught?" and later, "Can the germ run away?"

As the discussion progressed, Michael introduced the idea that there were different kinds of white blood cells, "markers" or those that discovered germs, and "eaters" or those that attacked them. Toward the end of the discussion, Bill used that idea, characterizing white blood cells as "watch dogs" and "hit men." The discussion introduced a great deal of new and very specific information, for example, about pus, plasma, and how immunities are built up. After Michael left, the children spent time throughout the day looking at the books and pictures he had brought and viewing the slides of blood under a microscope. The next day I asked the children to draw a new picture about their question, showing an idea that had been important to them.

Figure 8.2 shows the kinds of drawings the children produced. They were very different from their first drawings. What was immediately striking was the new kind of knowledge the children were working with. The notion of blood as somehow controlling the brain was completely gone, and, instead, every drawing focused on some aspect

Figure 8.1 Three Children's Drawings After the First Talk About the Question "What Is Blood For?"

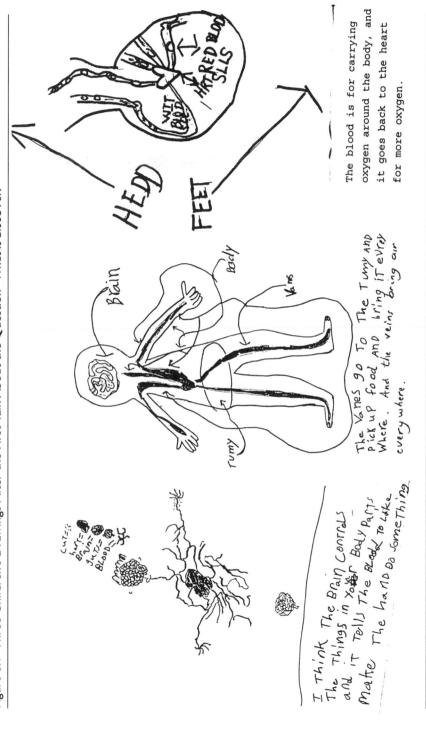

HEDD

FEET

WITE BLOOD

HARED BLOOD SLLS

The blood is for carrying oxygen around the body, and it goes back to the heart for more oxygen.

Brain

Body

Vens

Tumy

The vens go to the tumy and pick up food and bring it every where. And the veins bring air every where.

CUTS=
haat=
BRAIN=
JUST=
BLOOD=

I think the brain controls the things in your body parts and it tells the blood to make the hand do something

Figure 8.2 Three Children's Drawings After Michael's Visit About the Question "What Is Blood For?"

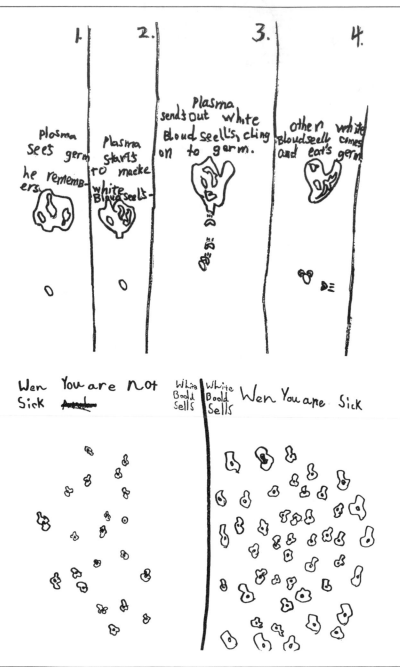

Figure 8.2 continued

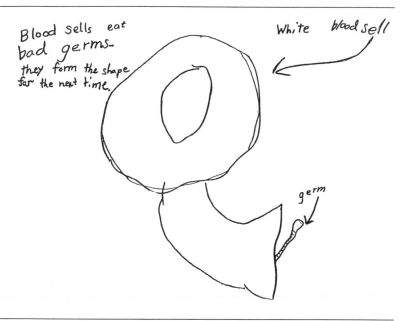

Blood sells eat bad germs. they form the shape for the next time.

White blood sell

germ

of the structure of blood. The children's prior understanding of white and red blood cells as a simple two-part system, had expanded to include the idea that there were different kinds of red and white cells with different functions in keeping the body healthy. As Ricky wrote: "Plasma is like a oracle or a wise man. It remembers everything. When a germ comes that it knows, it makes markers. The markers chase the germs and cling to the germs."

WHAT DO CHILDREN KNOW ABOUT HUMAN BIOLOGY?

It is interesting for me, when looking back on the work that these children did over more than a year of inquiry around their own questions, that the theories they developed about the human body go well beyond the developmental expectations for children of this age. Essentially, cognitive scientists tell us that children 6, 7, and 8 years old move from believing that internal organs are separate entities, each having "a static function: the heart is for love, the lungs are for breathing, the stomach is for eating, and the brain is for thinking," to articulating how each organ helps to move different substances throughout the body: "The organs are all containers, with channels of various sorts (e.g., blood vessels) connecting them" (Carey, 1985, pp. 47–48). It is only later, at around age 10, that children begin to develop metabolic or cellular theories of how the body works. (See Carey, 1985, for a review of the literature on children's understandings of the human body.)

The children in my class certainly began with some age appropriate understandings, but their level of theorizing began at what Carey calls the "container" function (p. 48). As the early talks on bones and brain showed, the children initially saw the body as a system in which things were moved from one place to another by the blood. However, their early ideas were far more developed than one would expect from cognitive researchers' studies of children's understandings (again, see Carey, 1985, pp. 41–71).

For example, in speaking about the brain, different children stated that the brain controlled all of the body. Some said this happened through "little tubes," "little signals," or "brain pipes," and even though they incorrectly attributed the movement of the messages to the blood, their theory established that the brain controlled the body: "The brain does control your body, but the blood rules it." Even prior to our extended work on blood, as a group these children attributed much of the body's work to the action of cells and metabolic processes, an achievement that researchers had associated with children age 10 and up.

It is difficult for me to say why there is such a discrepancy between the thinking of a group of 6, 7, and 8 year olds in my setting and the findings of cognitive researchers over several decades. Perhaps the differences might lie in the population of the children I teach or in their exposure to books and resources in the school and home. Another explanation might lie in the starting point of the children's questions. *When they initiated these talks, they did not naturally ask about the characteristics of individual organs; they asked "how" questions.* They wanted to know the dynamics of a system, rather than the isolated operation, of, say, the heart.

Further, their ideas on these questions weren't solicited on an individual basis, but rather were developed by the children themselves as a group in a Science Talk. Thus, as in most of the Science Talks, the theories that emerged were collective theories, and they were much more powerful and dynamic because of that collaborative work. Many ideas were reconciled into an emergent theory, and at no time was a theory entertained that did not view the body as an integrated system. I also believe that these theories developed to a more sophisticated level because the children, in talking together, developed cogent metaphors that enabled them to conceptualize very difficult ideas.

TALK AS A STARTING POINT FOR STUDY

I should point out that at no time did I view this work on the human body as completely within my control. The questions began to be asked, and when I finally realized they represented a train of thought by an entire class, a unit of study was unfolding with minimal planning by me. The children were clearly in control of the pacing and resources for their study. I added books, arts experiences, an outside expert, and knowledge when it was asked for. The central focus of this unit, however, was talk and the times when we came together to process new information or discuss a new question.

Obviously, in looking at the evolution of the children's theories, a great deal of talking and thinking took place outside of my observation. Investigations into one question inevitably led to newer and more complex questions. For example, the question, "What is blood for?" progressed naturally to, "How is blood made?"; "How does the brain work?" moved on to "Why, when you pinch yourself, does it hurt?" The content of the children's deep interest in human biology was completely linked to their opportunities to talk together about those interests. My role consisted of staying out of their way in the sense that I had to avoid imposing my own ideas as to how they "ought" to proceed in their explorations, and orchestrating follow-up experiences that helped them to work with new ideas, test new theories, or search for the answers to more difficult questions. I also took on a very important role, when it was necessary, of coaching them as talkers. The story of that process will be told in the next chapter.

CHAPTER 9

Teacher as Model, Teacher as Coach

ANDY: (whispering to me) Remember I didn't used to do these, but now I do.

T: Andy just made a comment that before he didn't use to do these Science Talks in first grade, but now he's doing more. Hmm, wonder why that is.

ANDY: You know, second graders.

T: (laughs) You know, second graders!

ANDY: Before I was the one that didn't say a word. But I kept on saying little ones. *They* used to say a lot. Now I'm saying more than they are!

This chapter is titled as if the teacher is really in charge of the Science Talks. I want to state clearly that this is only slightly true. The teacher has the power to establish Science Talks as a regular practice in a classroom, but the teacher is never in charge of the outcome of the talks, either at a conceptual level or from a linguistic standpoint.

When I first started Science Talks, and really began to be quiet in them, I quickly realized that I could not control the direction and style of the talks without undoing the power adjustment that they originally had been intended to remedy. As I mentioned in Chapter 1, there is a "power asymmetry" in the classroom (Edwards & Mercer, 1987), and that imbalance often leaves the teacher in a position of not being able to assess what children know and don't know, and the child in a position of never fully appropriating a discourse.

I found in the early talks that I was unaccustomed both to the children's style of talking and to many of their metaphorical and analogical uses of language. More often than not, it seemed that the talks were disorderly or "messy," a trait I now know characterizes exploratory talk. When I began to look carefully at the transcripts of the talks, however, and saw that the children's theories were constructed logically and carefully, I was able to tolerate the pace and style of the talks. I also learned that in any Science Talks there are two things that the teacher must carefully watch *and* reflect upon: the science content of the talks *and* the talk behaviors of the children.

For the first 2 years of my work with Science Talks, I was fortunate to have classes of children that seemed to know a great deal about talking together in positive and productive ways. I was able to document the characteristics of very good Science Talks, and the kinds of talk behaviors many of those children naturally exhibited. I saw many talks in which children listened carefully to each other, referred to earlier statements, asked clarifying questions, and disagreed with each other *respectfully*. I saw how collaborative talk could gradually lure even the most quiet children into the conversation.

However, the next 3 years of Science Talks introduced me to new issues in looking at Science Talks: language and power. I believe these issues moved to the foreground because of a subtle change in the composition of my classes. Although the classes continued to represent diverse populations, there was a subtle change in the ratio of boys to girls and in the discourse styles of the boys in the classes.

After 2 years with talented science talkers, I noted that the following year the boys were becoming increasingly more dominant, although there were still a few powerful second grade girls who maintained a strong presence in the talks and made sure that the talks were not dominated by any individuals or groups of children. The following September, 10 first graders from the prior year stayed with me and were joined by 12 new second graders.

By October I realized that there was a very powerful and closed group of Caucasian boys, all of whom had been with me the previous year, who dominated all the Science Talks. (They also attempted to control other areas of classroom discourse.) Only one of the girls in the class chose to participate in the Science Talks, and new second grade boys who had come in from other schools or classes were also silent.

As the weeks passed, and I observed that the other children were not able, *or willing*, to break into the talks, I began to work with the whole class on their respective talk behaviors. The entire fall of that school year was devoted to helping these children look at their own talk behaviors. I believe the teacher's role as a model and a coach can be clearly presented by describing the development of this class of children and documenting the insights they themselves articulated about how to change the dynamics of their talks.

OCTOBER: ESTABLISHING TALK PROTOCOLS

In early October of that year, the class discussed the question, "How do babies grow inside the mother?" This was our third Science Talk, and the first in which the pattern of interaction among the boys became clearly apparent. It opened with my request that two boys who had been extremely dominant try to maintain some silence: "People who talked a lot last time, Mike and Maurice, I want you to say one thing and then sit back and let the next person in." Within 30 seconds, however, three boys, including those two, were talking simultaneously, leaving no opportunities for anyone else to enter the conversation. (Note that the use of brackets, [   ], here shows when children were talking at the same time as the first speaker.)

MIKE: It starts like, sort of like a small little ball, like a lead
[CHARLES: A seed.]
[MAURICE: A seed, yeah.]
MIKE: not exactly a seed, but
[CHARLES: Yeah, a little]
[MAURICE: Yeah.]
MIKE: a little ballish thing that looks kind of
[CHARLES: tiny thing]
MIKE: like a seed and then it kind of like gets little bumps on it
[CHARLES: It gets, and then]
MIKE: and then it grows,
[CHARLES: It shapes, it shapes.]
MIKE: it grows and then the bumps grow and then it shapes and
[CHARLES: our shapes come out.]
[MAURICE: and that's the way it starts.]
MIKE: then it grows and it's kind
T: Mike, after you end the sentence sit back.

With my intervention, another child tried to make a statement.

RICHARD: I think when the mother is eating the baby eats. The food
comes down in the belly.

But Maurice jumped aggressively on this remark, speaking quite loudly and in a perjorative tone.

MAURICE: Yeah, but Richard! And how would it get there in the first place?

I intervened once again and asked the boys to please be quiet. Each time another child made an attempt to add a new idea, the boys would question them aggressively or interject a loud "No!" However, they never questioned or objected to any of their own statements.

As the other children watched, five of the boys carried on a private conversation about the question, agreeing with each other and ignoring the statements of others. I had to continually prompt certain of the boys not to talk just to each other or to address their remarks to me. Much of the time they were all talking at once.

Finally Cindy, my intern, spoke: "I'm having a really difficult time because we have three or four people talking at once so I can't follow anyone's conversation. Listen to each other!" A little while later I stopped the talk once again and asked people who hadn't spoken to come in. Mia spoke, but no one responded to her idea. As the boys jumped to fill the space, I asked for more children, and Diane came in to agree with Mia, amplifying her idea. The boys did not respond. As silence fell, the boys began to talk again, and I noticed that Rachel, one of my most reticent girls, was making signs that she had something to say. I motioned her to speak.

RACHEL: I think how the baby breathes is through the oxygen cord.
T: The oxygen cord, that cord?
RACHEL: Yeah.
MAURICE: The baby wouldn't, really wouldn't be able to breathe
    when it wasn't formed yet!

The boys started talking again, agreeing with Maurice. Rachel and the other girls fell silent. Another child began to speak about Maurice's objection to Rachel's remark, disagreeing with him, but Maurice interrupted before he could finish his statement.

MAURICE: Yeah, that's what I was saying.
CHARLES: Yeah, its a seed, not an egg.
MAURICE: That's what I was saying.

A few minutes later, as the boys continued to talk about whether the "seed" could breathe, Germaine, an African-American child, developed the most effective metaphor of the talk. Germaine made four bids for attention, naming Maurice to get his attention, before Maurice offhandedly acknowledged him.

GERMAINE: Maurice. Maurice. Maurice. Maurice. I think how long
    the baby stays in the mother's stomach is how long it grows.

Germaine was interrupted by the three boys all at once, but he tried to continue.

GERMAINE: It's just like caterpillars.
T: Go ahead.
GERMAINE: It's just like caterpillars when they grow. They turn into butterflies. You know how butterflies grow? It makes more sense if the baby grows like butterflies.

As always when children are developing metaphors, I did not completely follow Germaine's thinking, but I had a hunch that it made sense, and I asked if anyone could help expand the idea. Of course, Mike volunteered, but Germaine was not done.

GERMAINE: You know how caterpillars grow, and they turn into, like, big caterpillars?

He was interrupted by Eli, another very vocal talker.

ELI: Yeah. Except Germaine, I don't get it.
T: Ask him a question. That way he can say more.
ELI: We don't turn into humans and fly you know.
T: How do you mean?
ELI: Well, maybe we fly airplanes, but besides that . . . [Eli shrugged and smiled broadly at the group.]
MAURICE: Yeah. I sort of agree with Eli.
CHARLES: I do, too.

Thus, Germaine's idea was dismissed.
    A few minutes later, Eli spoke again, beginning his statement with a subtle insult to Germaine.

ELI: Maybe, maybe, now we're more talking like it might make sense. Take a bird. First it's an egg. Then it gets more. Then it gets more feathers, more hair and gets bigger. Then it gets to be a grown-up bird.

Naturally the other boys took up this idea for 2 or 3 minutes and supported it, not acknowledging how Germaine's use of the caterpillar's metamorphosis had triggered Eli's bird image.
    Personally, I absolutely hated this talk. It was the first time that I clearly saw how the boys were silencing *all* of the other children by not

responding to their ideas and by leaving no spaces for other children to get in the talk. I had to take an extraordinarily active role in policing the amount of time that the boys talked, and that really irked me. At this point in time other children were still trying to speak, but the majority of the class was not participating. In my field notes, I entered a reminder for myself to remind the children to acknowledge other children's contributions.

> Perhaps I should note next time that if someone's idea triggers you to another thought, even if it's much later, you should give credit.

Our next Science Talk focused on the question, "How did animals start?" I opened the talk with the following remarks:

T: I want to ask, especially today, for the boys who talk a lot to not act like it's just a conversation between themselves. I feel when I watch sometimes that, first of all, no one else can get in. Because when you guys talk, the sentences go on and on and on. There's no spaces in your sentences. It's important that when you say one thing, you stop, and sit back, and let people think about it. And also let them get in. Do other people sort of agree with me? It's hard to get in.

MAURICE: It's hard for me to get in.

T: No, it's not hard for you to get in. You are one of the people who really needs to work on this.

However, as can be seen from what followed, the boys did not take my remarks seriously.

MIKE: Well, I think, that it really depends on what kind of animals, like reptiles, mammals, fish, really depends on what kind. 'Cause, like maybe, like, the first kind of animals were in the sea. But they probably weren't like fish; they probably were like reptiles.

CHARLES: Well, I think, probably, um, like, uh, like each baby was sort of like different

[MIKE: I know.]

CHARLES: and it came different, each baby if they had a baby, it

[MIKE: It came]

CHARLES: came different, looked different, and that may be how.

MAURICE: Like there are all different types of them, and when differ-

ent types made it, it made a different type from those two types,
cause they were a combination of those types, and it kept on
making more and more and more

MIKE: Yeah it kept on producing more and more and more of that
kind.

The conversation continued this way with these boys talking among
themselves, looking only at each other, interrupting and talking over
each other much as they had in the prior talk, and finally breaking out
into an argument over who, among them, was talking first.

After about 10 minutes, Cindy and I conferred, and Cindy made
an intervention, which I then built upon.

T2: You really need to look around the circle to see who is trying to
get a word in edgewise. When you are always just talking to one
person, if I'm always just talking to Maurice, and Tian has something to say, I'm never going to know that. Mia has been trying
to say something for quite awhile.

T: Let's give a couple of jobs to a couple of people. Mike, I'm giving
you a job. You can't talk. But you must look around, and when
you see someone who's trying to get in, you should point to that
person so we know. OK. I'm going to give you a job. Maurice,
same job. We have two lookers. This might be a way to help
people start to see. Now if you want to get in, you gotta give a
sign.

MAURICE: Can I go "Uh hum" (pointing to himself).

T: No. You can't do yourself. You have to be completely silent.

MIKE: You mean we can't speak!

T: Nope. You've got to watch. You've got to start looking and see
who wants to talk 'cause you aren't doing that.

Mike and Maurice begrudgingly took on their new role and the talk
was better in the sense that more children tried to join in.

In my field notes, I noted the following instructions for the children in the next talk:

1. If you don't understand what someone has said, you
could say "Do you mean . . . ?" and try to ask a specific
question.

The goal in that would be to help other people be clearer.

2. If you don't know how to get in, what are some signals
you give so other people would know?

The next scheduled talk was on the question, "What is science?" I
introduced the talk, outlining carefully what kinds of talk protocols we
wanted to think about.

> I want to read some things, notes that I made last week
> about our talking. You remember that we had some people
> last week not speaking but pointing out who wanted to
> speak. I would like to not do that again. I'd like those
> people to talk, but, but I won't be able to do it unless those
> people can think about their talk. I have instructions for
> those people. Instead of always, guys, of always jumping in
> and saying something else that somebody said, you should
> really listen to the person that goes ahead of you. See if you
> can add anything to what they say. Or if you don't under-
> stand what they mean, don't say, "I don't know what you
> mean," or, "That isn't so"; ask them a question to help them
> think a little bit more. It helps people if you say, for ex-
> ample, "Allen, do you mean . . . ?"

I then went on to discuss what children could do if they couldn't
get in. Predictably, the boys gave advice on how to do that.

ELI: You could look at the people who are talking so that they'll notice you.
MAURICE: You could raise your hand.
T: In fact, if you see someone, if you're a person who's talking but
also noticing that someone wants to get in and is kind of signaling, you should get the group to let that person in.

NOVEMBER: BREAKING INTO SMALLER GROUPS

As November began, even though the talks were still dominated
by what the children called the "big talkers," I made the following
entry in my field notes: "We are still having trouble orchestrating a
conversation, but more children are speaking. Now I can count silent
ones." I decided after this talk to do a series of listening exercises
within the context of the talks. The rules were: If you say something,
you choose the next talker, and that person must re-say what you said

and add to it. We used this tactic in the next talk, and it was a very slow and tedious process. I noted that all but one of the girls were silent the whole talk.

The next week our question was, "Does space ever end?" This time my list of who talked and who didn't was very discouraging. Of the 18 children who were present, 11 were not talking. The same four boys (Charles, Mike, Maurice, and Eli) dominated the conversation and were joined occasionally by two other boys and one girl.

Cindy and I decided to take more drastic measures. The following week we separated the talkers from the nontalkers and asked the talkers to draw a picture of their ideas about the question, "How is blood made?" The rest of the class had their own talk and did quite well. The girls were much more involved. Almost every child contributed to the talk. At the end of the talk, I asked the children who were in the talk how they thought it had gone.

T: How do you think this went? Was it better for you?
KATIE: 'Cause sometimes, some of the boys, Maurice and Mike, and Charles, they sort of laugh when, like, when some things, when we think it's done, or something, and they know the real answer, they laugh.
T: This is what I want you to know about Science Talks, for people who are a little shy. When we ask these questions, nobody in the class knows. If you don't know, you shouldn't think Maurice or Mike know. They don't know either. So they just, they just talk 'cause they're not shy.
GERMAINE: Because Mike acts like it's just him, talking. He don't let anybody else talk.
T: Well, we're working on that.

After the children went to lunch, I compared the pictures done by the big talkers with the theories that had been proposed by the other group. I realized that the big talkers didn't know any more than their silent peers, but rather had fancier trappings for their ideas. For example, most children thought blood was made from the food they ate, but the big talkers used words like "digestion" and "blood cells."

We followed the two-group model the next week as well, talking about the question, "Why, when you pinch yourself, does it hurt?" Cindy and I decided to repeat that same talk with the whole class the following week. We reasoned that the more reticent talkers had had a rehearsal, as it were, for the question, and the big talkers might have had some time to reflect upon their role in the talks. Further, when we showed the drawings from the blood question, and compared them with the theories the other children had built during their talk, the new talkers realized that many of their ideas were the same as those of the more dominant talkers.

DECEMBER: HOW LONG SHOULD WE WAIT?

For this talk the group was reunited and discussed the question from the prior week. My field notes from this talk describe my reaction.

> This time we are having the whole class talk together. Cindy and I both feel it's time to back up and let the talk unfold and see what happens. Who talks? Can the talkers *ever* be quiet? Mike asks to let others talk. Charles starts to talk, and then he says, "Oh, Kim, did you want to talk?" She says, "No." So far, 2 minutes in, only dominant boys are talking. Nate tries to join in, asks Maurice a question. Maurice then takes over and rambles on. What are other children doing? Nate tries to make his point about "pathways" to Maurice, but Maurice is too busy yacking to notice, so Nate says, "Oh, well" and stops talking. Boy, there was a world in that "Oh, well." One could translate it as: "Well, I guess he doesn't really care what I think, and it's probably not very important anyway, so I'll just be quiet." But then (hooray!) Mike hears that "Oh, well" and responds, so Nate does finish his idea.

The following day we listened to the tape of that Science Talk with the whole class. Looks were exchanged as the dominant talkers heard themselves. At the end, I asked the children if they had any reactions to the tape they had heard. Kim suggested that people who talk a lot should say, "I think" when they were giving an idea and that they should talk "a little less loud." She was very clear that loud talk was intimidating and "sounds like there's no other answer." Eli agreed with her. Mia proposed that "people should just pretend the talkers aren't there."

Mike suggested that the big talkers wait after they talked before they said anything else and that they not "talk again until someone silent has said something." Someone asked, "How long should we wait?" and Mike responded, "Ten seconds."

"No," said Eli. "Ten minutes."

We decided to take Eli's suggestion to heart. The next talk was on the question, "How was the earth made?" and we began with the idea that no big talker could speak until most of the "little talkers" had said something. The children all nodded their heads in agreement, and we waited. The tape recorder recorded a silence of 6½ minutes as the children sat. The big talkers were unusually calm and showed no impatience or agitation. They sat quietly, looking at their hands and occasionally at the other children. It was a respectful and relaxed silence.

At 2½ minutes I said, "You're doing a good job talkers," and we waited some more. Finally, in the sixth minute, Nate said, "Can someone talk?" and Mike added, "And we won't make fun of you." At that point, Germaine made a statement and the talk began. Although there were still silent children, the climate was very different. The big talkers were showing extraordinary restraint, and they were listening to the other children.

At the end of the talk, we discussed what the big talkers perceived to be a new problem, and I have to admit I agreed with them. Some children just wouldn't join in no matter how long we waited. A discussion ensued of what the quiet people could do. Mike thought perhaps we should tell them the question a day early so they could be ready. I pointed out that they also had to try to help with our talks, since so many other children were working hard to make the talks work. Germaine ended the discussion with this advice: "For you guys who don't know how to talk, go home and ask your mother."

JANUARY: REARRANGING POWER RELATIONSHIPS

Our first talk upon returning from the winter vacation was on a question Mia had asked, "What makes electricity?" When Cindy and I announced that it was time for Science Talks, the children literally ran to get ready in the meeting area, organizing themselves into a circle with unusual speed. Mia opened the discussion, and as I recorded who was contributing, I noted that we had three new talkers, all girls, and that there was much more attention to some of the talk protocols we had been working on. Children were crediting other children's ideas; they were waiting for new speakers to join in and ending their sentences in a timely fashion. Most important, the theory that emerged was constructed through the participation and tenacity of two formerly silent girls.

At the end of the talk, I questioned the class about what had made this talk work.

T: What happened, what did you see?
MIKE: Like, um, if we said one thing we wouldn't say, "and also . . . ." Yeah, we'd just like, stop and let someone else get in and come back later.
TIAN: Well, like, for example, first of all when all the other nontalkers talked, the big talkers couldn't get in much and it could be much evener.
KIM: It's kind of like all the soft talkers that don't talk so much jumped in.
NATE: The soft talkers said more and that helped the big talkers.

From January into February, the children took control of their own talk behaviors. The talks that followed were much more balanced. Children who hadn't participated began to make brief forays into the middle of the talks. Cindy and I pulled out of the coaching role and we found that the formerly dominant talkers would prompt their friends when they were slipping back into old roles: "Say, 'I think'"; "Remember to say one thing and wait." Charles, especially, began to talk in a new way. He changed from making assertions about the question to using "maybe" before a statement, and his ideas were voiced with a marvelous tone of wonder and awe. As that change took place, he moved into expressing much more original, and often outlandish, ideas and no longer spent his time revoicing his friends' remarks. It seemed as if in the process of abdicating some of his social power, he had gained an ability to really speak about his own, very imaginative ideas.

One wonders to what extent this work of rearranging power relationships in a group of talkers is liberating for those who are essentially powerless and voiceless, as well as for the children who hold a lock on that power. Certainly it freed me up to reassume the role I prefer in these talks, that of observer and occasional participant. When I saw that this class was actually beginning to talk together without my intervention, I realized that the explicit work on talk behaviors and talk protocol that had so permeated our Science Talks that fall had worked for this group of children.

I began to see changes in other areas of the classroom. The children became very concerned about a few boys and girls who never participated in any discussions or sharing of work. Serious parlays were held as to what the class could do about those children. There was a consensus that silence was not acceptable because it meant that "the same people were always doing all of the thinking work." As the dominant children became clearer on that point, they began to use some of their energy to persuade quieter people to be less shy.

Gradually, as the year progressed, these reticent children experimented with more public kinds of talk. More children participated in sharing time. Completely shy and silent girls, including new English speakers, started to read entries from their science journals to the class and responded to questions and comments. Formerly silent girls plotted together to find ways to get their still silent friend to speak in Science Talks. They consulted with me regularly and gave her pep talks before the talks. I watched girls who had been terrified of speaking in Science Talks become active and vociferous theory builders, and I witnessed Mike, Charles, and sometimes even Maurice giving up the floor graciously and attentively to other, less extroverted talkers.

FEBRUARY: REPHRASING THE QUESTIONS

Many children more openly stated their naive theories, allowing Cindy and I to work with their ideas in our science lessons, and new questions emerged from formerly silent girls. The first of those questions was worded very differently from prior questions. "How do dreams get into our heads?" two girls asked, and we put the question to the group for a talk in mid-February. It had a remarkable effect. Every child but two talked with extreme interest and energy. Rachel, formerly the most reticent of the silent girls, opened the talk and led the discussion at different points, even interrupting the group at one point to ask a very pointed question of another child.

As the children talked, they began to move closer to one another, and the circle got smaller as they went on. I noted in my field notes: "They look like they're *really* talking to each other!" Only one child was notably silent, and that was Maurice. He tried halfheartedly to get in and then gave up because the other children were so vocal. I wondered later in my notes what had happened to make this talk so active and successful.

Perhaps it was the question. Because everyone had clearly thought about this, and had a theory. Their theories eventually blended into one. I wonder now, will they all participate in a less familiar question?

The next week, Cindy and I reconsidered the dynamics of the prior talk. We were certain by that time that the phrasing of the question had had a large effect. When the girls used the inclusive wording, "How do dreams get into *our* heads?" instead of saying, "Where do dreams come from?" it seemed as if every child was invited to contribute his or her personal idea. So we took the next question, "What is gravity?" which had been asked by one of the more vocal boys a few weeks earlier, and rephrased it, "Why, when you jump, do you come down?"

After doing a few jumps in place to frame the question, we opened it up for discussion. Mia immediately put an idea on the floor, and other children joined in. Then Mike said the answer was "gravity." Before Cindy or I could ask him to define that term, Latia whispered to Cindy: "I don't get it. What does gravity have to do with jumping?" She said it in such a way that Cindy knew the word "gravity" was a new one for her. Cindy asked her to say the question out loud, and when she did, all of the big talkers tried to continue the use of the term. Some said gravity was like a "gas," and others tried to give examples of gravity, explaining how if you threw a ball it came back to earth, but it was clear that none of them had a working definition that would further the group's discussion. Finally, the term was dropped and the children went on to build a theory about the role of weight in determining what would fall down.

The talk proceeded energetically with the same participation as the week earlier, and when we were finished I realized that the gradual change in the talk climate had enabled me to learn both about how to develop the talk behaviors of a class, as well as something new about the way science questions are phrased.

When the question about dreams surfaced, it was phrased in a way that had meaning to every child in the class and allowed all children to participate. After 5 years of watching Science Talks, I was able to see from the development of this class as talkers that even the phrasing of a question, whether asked by an adult or a child, can silence (and thereby exclude) some children who have less experience in the "coined" terminology of science.

Further, I saw that those children who have had more exposure to the technical language of science and often can speak with authority because they use those terms, rarely understood the meaning of the terms even though they often applied them in the correct contexts. Words such as "chemical," "nutrition," and "cells" in some ways limited those children's ability to *really* talk about a new question. While some children did, indeed, use those words to build organizing concepts, as I described in Chapter 6, others used the words to provide quick answers without any substance behind them. As all of the children in the class realized that this was true, they no longer blindly accepted the use of the terminology. If a word was used that they did not recognize or understand, they would ask for a meaning, for example, "What does 'process' mean?" or "I don't get what you mean by 'nutrition.'"

This new behavior spilled over into other subjects. For example, in book discussions, new and even "big" talkers would stop the discussion by asking for the meaning of a word used by another child or a teacher; a movement session would be interrupted by a child who insisted on knowing the meaning of a key word. Silence was replaced by a commitment from almost every child to defining our terms so that everyone could participate in every activity.

As I watched the changes in this class, I remembered the silence of my own childhood and was so thankful that these children had assumed some responsibility for raising the voices of all of their classmates. I hoped that their new awareness of the vigor and excitement that real collaborative talk produces would become addictive so that they would never let so many voices fall silent again. Certainly the sound of your own voice is a very compelling thing, but the sound of your voice with many others is far more transformative.

CHAPTER 10

You Could Make a Song About Science

Since the talk on "Why is the ocean salty?" Germaine has been asking me daily, "Can we talk about the salt water today?" I can't
fathom what this means. Is it that he wants to do more Science
Talks, or that he is inordinately fascinated by salt water? Think I'll ask.
—From my field notes, Oct. 4

T: You say to me every day for 2 weeks almost, "Are we going to talk
  about salt water today?" What does that question mean? What is
  it that you're trying to find out from me?
GERMAINE: I like talking about something. I like hearing about salt
  water.
T: What is it you like hearing about the salt water stuff? You really
  liked the salt water talk, 'cause I remember that you talked in
  that talk, right?
GERMAINE: I thinked about a answer. That's how I talked.
T: Is it the salt part you like, or is it the talk?
GERMAINE: (almost inaudible) The talk . . . (louder) Salt water.
T: The salt water part. Why the salt water part? (I missed the first
  low words, "The talk," until I listened to the tape.)

This exchange marked the first of my conversations with and observations of Germaine in and around Science Talks. At first my direct
questions to him were confusing for both of us. I wondered what was
happening for Germaine as he continued to focus on this one question.
He, in turn, was probably mystified by my desire to understand his
meaning, volunteering as he did in this conversation both possible answers. However, by the end of October, I was pretty well convinced
that Germaine's interest went beyond salt water. He would race to be
first to Science Talks, and often after a talk would give Cindy or myself
a huge bear hug of joy and excitement.

As the year progressed, Germaine began to pop with questions. He would turn to me in the middle of a reading group and say, "I have a question. How did the sun get that round shape?" By December, everyone he came in contact with heard new questions: "Why is grass green?"; "How was glass made?"; "How *do* those butterflies grow when they're in that cocoon thing?" Germaine was showing me what I had always suspected. Every child has boundless questions that, once loosed, proliferate almost uncontrollably. Further, when the questions are valued and honored in the child's classroom community, *the child's desire to know becomes translated into an identification with the subject he or she questions.*

Germaine came to my classroom silent and apparently unfamiliar with the science materials that were available there. I know he had had interesting experiences in first grade because he referred to his work with caterpillars and meal worms. But as a student of science, Germaine was very passive. When I realized that Germaine could not observe the newts as they swam in their tank because he didn't know what a newt was, even though they were swimming in front of him, I took the newts out of their tank for him to hold. He was awkward and afraid of those tiny creatures, just as he was interested in but unwilling to touch Violet, our bunny. My explanations of why it was so important to watch these animals and think about what they were doing, or to handle other materials, seemed to have little effect. Germaine held himself apart from the other children's excitement about science and, except for his enthusiasm about Science Talks, he showed little interest in science work.

But something about the practice of Science Talks pulled him in. After 3 months, he began to throw out questions during the course of every day. Those questions were garnered from the books he read, from the experiences he had both in and out of school, and from his imagination. By January, when we talked about a question Germaine had asked, "How did the sun begin?" he proposed what some of the other children took to be an outrageous idea—that there was no reason the sun had to be round. "It coulda started in a box, or in a square shape," he stated firmly, provoking the confusion and uproar that many outrageous, but important, statements always trigger in our Science Talks.

Amid the uproar, other, quieter children joined Germaine in his theory. Why, they asked, did people always say the sun was round? How could we know the real shape of the sun when it started, or even now if we couldn't get close to it? That action on Germaine's part signaled his movement into the world of science. It was the result of both his serious desire to understand the endeavor I was asking him to join and my wish to help him take on some of the identity of the scientist: to bring his experiences in the city into our classroom, to speak with conviction about his ideas, to ask questions, and hopefully in the end to join us fully in our explorations with materials and experiments.

I wish that for all of the children I teach. I wish that every child would desire to know about the world in a boundless and wondering way, and that every child would believe that he or she could engage in conversations and investigations about that world *with pride*, rather than hesitation. I believe that if that could happen for every child, we would discover that many children have the ability to study science with intelligence and skill. That shift alone would change the face of science as it is conceptualized and practiced. It would become a discipline where our understanding of the world would come to include the viewpoints of many cultures and races, and both genders.

CONSTRUCTING A DISCOURSE

That change, however, requires a careful reconsideration of how children are taught science. In this book I have attempted to take a close look at one aspect of that teaching and to describe how an expansion of our understanding of science talk might re-orient and realign both the teaching of science and the balance of power among those who can speak with authority about it in the classroom.

If we return to a reconsideration of the notion of "appropriation" as Bakhtin described it, the very subtle link between the language of a discipline and the practice of it becomes clear. When as a teacher I strive to have each child be admitted to conversations about the world of science, I am hoping to help all children find a way to own, or appropriate, some understanding of the language, attitude, mind, and psyche of the scientist. I am working to extend scientific literacy to all children by attending to the construction of a discourse in my classroom. I don't care about what children's native potential is or whether they are gifted or just normal. I care that all children feel included in the discussion and that all children feel the power of collaborative theory building and in fact understand the excitement of building a theory, *even if it is an incorrect theory.* Incorrect theories are better than no theories at all! Incorrect theories are better than silence! Incorrect theories are, in fact, often the basis for correct and revolutionary theories in the field of science.

UNCOVERING CHILDREN'S THEORIES

When we strive to uncover children's theories, we see how they are constructed and as a result can more carefully construct our own teaching. For example, we can identify children's carefully developed misconceptions. I see from my work in the classroom that misconceptions are not always hastily put together. They are the result of observation, imagination, and logic; their development is the result of careful, though informal, scientific inquiry and is yet another example of children's natural predisposition for scientific thinking.

Rather than viewing misconceptions as cause for distress and immediate intervention, we should carefully elicit them and work with the children to uncover the kinds of data upon which they have based their theories. Often the observations of nature that form the underpinnings of children's misconceptions have been carefully, and even systematically, noted in the child's mind. We can use that information, combining it with other experimental and observational experiences, to help children reconstruct their theories and expand their questions.

UNCOVERING CHILDREN'S QUESTIONS

Thus, there is in this book an orientation toward the teacher's commitment to readjusting the "power asymmetry" of the classroom by maintaining a modicum of silence in the Science Talks so that we can hear children's naive theories and uncover their deeper questions. If teachers are constantly interrupting children's conversations about the world, then the children eventually will not have those conversations in the teacher's presence. They will believe that their ideas are always being judged and are, most probably, not the right ideas. When they are asked questions, they will search the teacher's face for the right answer, modifying their response at even the slightest nonverbal reaction. The answers they do provide will be the teacher's or the textbook's answer, rather than their own.

When we make a space for children to talk to one another without our constant control over the talk, we begin to hear children's correct *and* incorrect thinking. We also assign a new value to children's questions by giving them a place of importance in the curriculum. In this way we see the seminal questions that, if left unsaid, may interfere with the goals of our teaching. We also will see more complex questions arise: "How did rice begin?"; "Is voice matter?" and we can develop curricula that mesh with the children's sense of wonder. These are rich sources of learning, debate, and challenge for all children and their teachers.

When we begin to think of curricula as emerging from children's questions and employ both directed *and* unintrusive strategies of instruction (see Chapter 8), the science curriculum moves more naturally into the communal life of the classroom. It becomes part of the process of building a community of scientists whose laboratory is the classroom and *whose interests, questions, and theories emerge from the inside-out, rather than the outside-in.* Science instruction from children's questions requires teachers to attend more to the natural rhythm of children's intellectual development. Rather than studying science only in designated time periods over the course of a week, the children think, talk, and do science all the time! And the ways that they do that work gain complexity, depth, and momentum as time passes.

RECOVERING CREATIVITY, IMAGINATION, AND WONDER

When teaching and learning about science are oriented toward children's agency—that is, when they begin with children's questions and theories and proceed more on their timetable—we can observe that children naturally express their theories, and sometimes their questions, about the world in metaphoric terms.

"Plasma is like a oracle." (Ricky, in Chapter 8)
"Is voice matter?" (Ellen, in Chapter 7)
"Blood is thicker [than water]. . . . It can hold blood cells. That's
    probably about as heavy as leaves." (Ian, in Chapter 8)
"The earth, sun, and moon are kind of like magnetic marbles."
    (Michael, in Chapter 4)

These images are not throwaway terms. They often help children "make the intellectual leap toward theory" (Gallas, 1994, p. 102) that they are not otherwise able to articulate using everyday language. When Germaine states that a baby grows "like a caterpillar," he is implying that a tremendous metamorphosis takes place in the mother's womb, not unlike the metamorphosis he remembers from his first grade year. He does not have the detailed knowledge of what exactly unfolds in utero; he cannot state it as succinctly as I might like so that I could better understand it, but he has some knowledge that he attempts to place within a powerful theory about development. I do not think he would have been capable of such a comparison if he had not engaged in Science Talks.

An understanding of the complexities of children's metaphors and the ways they naturally choose to explore their understandings of difficult concepts through more symbolic narratives enables teachers to "reclaim the child's mind" (see Chapter 6). If we explore the kinds of thinking elementary children are capable of, we cannot help but wish we had the same capacity ourselves. When we are able to resurrect our own wonder and our natural imaginative response to the world, we can better teach our children, understanding as we do that "final form science" is not where science begins, but rather is an outcome that has wrongly been inserted into the education of our children. Science does not originate from distance and objectification of the world of nature: It begins with wonder, imagination, and awe. As Germaine so aptly states: "You could sing a song about science." The separation of creativity, imagination, and wonder from the pursuit of science is artificial and disruptive to the development of children of *any* age.

RECLAIMING THE CHILD'S MIND

This is not easy work. The practice of Science Talks as I have described it is only one part of classroom science, and, as I have discovered, the questions children ask and want to talk about are closely tied to the kinds of materials and experiences they have in the classroom. Yet many teachers, like myself, have been convinced that we are not good at science and certainly are not capable of developing original curriculum in response to children's questions without help from "experts." Often, however, the curricula and the kits that the experts present to teachers are heedless of children's questions, development, and potential as thinkers, and make assumptions about the kinds of experiences they have had before coming to school. Curriculum units are mandated to be taught without any knowledge of the circumstances of the lives of the children I teach.

How can Germaine study about "The Seashore" if he's never been to one? How can he begin to speak and participate in a unit on "Pets" if he's never had one? When we talk about "Growth," and a child refers to "the holes inside homemade bread" to explain that bread "grows" before it is cooked, Germaine is appalled. He's never eaten homemade bread: The bread he eats doesn't have holes. Another child cross-references that remark by citing "the holes in Swiss cheese." Germaine, now completely at sea, says, "What's Swiss cheese?" If we, as teachers, don't begin to develop the science curriculum based on our knowledge of the children we teach, how will *all* of our students ever be fully engaged in the world of science?

Germaine needs to make the bread, eat the cheese, have the pets, and go to the seashore with his class and his teacher! As his teacher, I have to figure out how to help him bring his rich observations of the city and his spontaneous questions into our study of science. Germaine has many things to say about his world. I must provide an environment where Germaine can ask his questions and express his ideas, and then experience rich responses to those questions. These responses to his questions take the form of a well provisioned classroom, of carefully conceived experiments and ongoing explorations, of times when the children talk together and explore the nature of their thinking. Only then can I do more for Germaine and each of the other children I teach.

Through Science Talks we can invite all children into the discussion of science and the development of curriculum. I believe that in that process we can begin to rearrange all power relationships, both those that develop within a classroom community and those that are embedded in the very structure of schools. The classroom is simply a microcosm of the larger society. The rearrangements I speak of address issues of inequity in all areas of the classroom and the outside culture: issues of race, class, gender, and culture, and the more subtle social dynamics of "intelligence" and "fitness" for higher order work in our society.

I would propose that in carefully considering and reflecting on the language of science, in trying to understand how we might reconstruct the study of science in the classroom, we also consider how that reconstruction within the microcosm of the school might, eventually, reconfigure the field of science as a whole. Rather than having our children exclude themselves from the world of science at an early age, we might raise a generation of children that claim, celebrate, and then transform the practice and function of science in the next century.

Science Talk Questions

1. How did the moon begin?
2. Why is the earth a rounded shape?
3. Why does "science" exist?
4. Why is the center of the earth hot?
5. How are earthquakes made?
6. How did people learn to talk?
7. Where did the water come from?
8. What makes electricity?
9. How did the universe begin?
10. Why is it hot at the equator?
11. Why do the leaves change color?
12. How did plants begin?
13. How, and why, does the earth turn?
14. What makes lightning?
15. How do mirrors work?
16. Will the water ever dry up?
17. Will we ever be able to live on another planet?
18. How did rice plants begin?
19. Why do the seasons change?
20. How did the dinosaurs die?
21. What makes colors in nature?
22. How did "nature" begin?
23. Does the universe end?
24. Where does metal come from?
25. Is there life on other planets?
26. How does blood work?
27. How did animals begin?
28. How do our bones stay together?
29. Why do your eyes change shape?
30. How is a volcano made?
31. How do people age?
32. How does the brain work?
33. How did things get their names?
34. Is voice matter?
35. What makes the wind?
36. Why do animals change color in the winter or summer?
37. Are dragons real?
38. How were the first rocks made?
39. What makes snow white?
40. How do waves form?
41. What color were the dinosaurs?
42. What is too slow for the eye to see?
43. Why is it summer when the sun is further away from the earth, and winter when it is close?
44. Why does ice float?
45. Why is the ocean salty?
46. What makes rain?
47. How do babies grow inside the mother?
48. How do legs move?
49. How is blood made?
50. Why, when you pinch yourself, does it hurt?
51. Why are blood veins different colors?
52. How do plants grow?
53. Why are there planets in space?
54. How did Saturn get its rings?
55. Why do people die?
56. How do people grow?
57. How did dinosaurs begin?

58. Why, when you jump, do you come back down?
59. How do shells grow?
60. How do dreams get in our heads?
61. How did the sun begin?
62. How is a seed made?
63. Why don't birds have teeth?
64. How are rainbows made?
65. How did people begin?

Two Science Talks

"HOW DID THE MOON BEGIN?"—Grades I and 2

T: Today we're discussing Holly's question, "How did the moon begin?" meaning, how did it get made? Okay, and last time, really a lot of people helped us out here. Let's see what happens this time . . .

HOLLY: I think that the moon is made because there's like a lot of stars put together. Like during the day sometimes the moon's not out because the stars come away from the moon, or something, and, and at night when it gets a little darker, it turns into a moon, and, and then some stars go like, if there was a half a moon, like, and then, there's a whole moon, and then, some stars would go away and stay out out so, it could be, so some people could see the stars.

SHELLY: I think maybe, this is partly what I think, that um, I think partly some of it is some rock, like formed as a, a big circle out of the moon you know, so, maybe . . .

T: You agree to that part of Holly's, but you think it might have something to do with rock?

DONALD: I think maybe it's like, uh, it's like some kind of planet, planet or something, or star or something. Um, exploded or something, and like a white dwarf.

AMY: I think the moon got made by many little, sticky, like stuff that's called particles . . .

?: Yeah.

AMY: that are stuck together. I think they were very sticky, and then they stuck together, and then just, they formed into a circle.

T: Is that kinda like yours?

HOLLY: Uh

T: Or yours?

TOM: I think that stars are shiny white things.

BRANDY: I think that, um, a, a long time ago, there was a rock, and something like, maybe something from outer space, the air or something, came down and pulled it out, and the stars got mixed in with it you know, and it was like rocky, and the stars got mixed in with it you know and it made circle shapes.

T: made kind of circle shapes, do you want to speak, speak up to everybody . . .

ANDY: I think there's this rock before people were made and it started bursting open, and it got so shiny, and I think that we called it the moon.

HOLLY: I think that, that a lot of wet crystals, 'cause there was a big huge huge rock, and it blew up and a lot of crystals came out of it and then crystals turned into the moon. And, and then it like, and, it would change, and it would, like, take off half the crystals a day, and I think the stars were made out of crystals.

(long pause)

ELLEN: I think the moon was made out of gases.

?: Oh, yeah.

(Small disruption as many voices respond.)

T: Can you talk about that?

TOM: Then how can you walk on the moon?

T: Let her talk.

ELLEN: Like the sun.

ANDY: Then how can you walk? You can walk on the moon.

SHELLY: Yeah it's probably gases and rocks formed together.

?: Yeah, yeah.

T: And so you think maybe, maybe originally it had something to do with gases?

MANY: Yeah! (Chorus)

ELLEN: Maybe gases around it.

DONALD: Like the ring around Saturn.

T: Like the ring around Saturn, Donald says, and Tom asked a good question which was to say, if it's gases how could you walk on it? But maybe that's you know . . .

SHELLY: It's also rocks.

T: Yeah.

ELLEN: Well, I forgot that people could walk on the moon.

T: But it's a good question 'cause then you have to say, "oh yeah, well," and then as Shelly says "maybe it's gas and rocks," and like Donald says the rings are not just gas, there's stuff mixed in. It's a very good idea, Ellen kind of threw in there.

DONALD: Space planets that was made of gases inside.

T: Yeah. Donald just said like the, like the planet, like a planet that was made, Tom, of gases inside and it kinda mixed together, you could walk on the planet.

DONALD: Yeah.

T: In the beginning?

ELLEN: And there's something on the moon that I know. That there are craters made from the sky. They made a rabbit on the moon.

T: the shape of a rabbit.

ELLEN: Yeah.

T: that we can see.

ELLEN: I can see.

T: Yeah . . .

SHELLY: Somebody else told that to my mother.

?: I see it.

TOM: It's not the shape of a rabbit.

ELLEN: Yes, it is.

T: It's like, it's like when we look at it, it looks like a rabbit from far away?

BRANDY: You know the ?? It's, that that person told us that we can see the shape of a rabbit.

T: In the moon.

?: Yeah I think in the moon.

SAM: Oh yeah, yeah, I know that.

T: Did you know that? Amy?

AMY: I know how the moon's light is made.

T: Could you tell us that 'cause I don't know.

AMY: The sun shines through the moon and makes the light.

SAM: Oh yeah, you're right.

DONALD: I knew that. Yeah, it says so in my book. . . . It, like, reflects on the moon . . . no . . . something, something reflects on it, like, the sun shines on the moon and the moon shines down.

T: So that's, you knew that? The sun shines on the moon, and then the moon reflects to earth . . .

TONY: I knew that, before he said it.

SHELLY: I read that in a book once.

AMY: If there wasn't any sun, then the moon wouldn't shine.

T: If there wasn't any sun, the moon wouldn't shine.

SAM: No way.

T: No way, says Sam.

SHELLY: I read that in a book once, actually, but I had forgotten all about it.

T: But you had forgotten. It's nice to have someone remind you of it. Now sometimes these questions are really hard, so why don't, after we're done talking about this, we think of ways that we can find out the answer to these questions. If we want to find out the answer to the question, "How did the moon begin?" how should we find it out, what are some of the ways we could find out?

SAM: I don't know.

T: Well, let's brainstorm.

ELLEN: Ask a scientist.

T: We could ask a scientist, or . . .

ANDY: Eat a scientist.

SHELLY: Wait until I'm a scientist, and ask me.

T: Okay we've got, ask a scientist, or we could wait till Shelly's a scientist 20 years from now, and we could ask her. What else could we do? Donald says, Andy, that he has a book at home. Can he bring in some books? Okay, any other ideas?

"HOW DO BABIES GROW INSIDE THE MOTHER?"—Grade 2

T: People who talked a lot last time, Mike and Maurice, I want you to say one thing, and then sit back and let the next person in.

MAURICE: I think that babies form from food but they don't really get the same color as the food. That's what they're formed by.

CHARLES: Well . . . it st-, it starts from a little seed. That's one thing I know.

MIKE: It starts like, sort of like a small little ball, like an egg

[CHARLES: A seed]

MIKE: not exactly a seed, but

[CHARLES: Yeah, a little]

[MAURICE: Yeah.]

MIKE: a little ballish thing that looks kind of

[CHARLES: tiny thing.]

MIKE: like a seed and then it kind of like gets litle bumps on it

[CHARLES: It gets, and then]

MIKE: and then it grows,

[CHARLES: It shapes, it shapes]

MIKE: it grows and then the bumps grow and then it shapes and

[CHARLES: Our shapes come out.]

[MAURICE: and that's the way it starts.]

MIKE: then it grows and it's kind

T: Mike, after you end the sentence, sit back. And end the sentence. Jump in, Richard. Jump in, anyone.

RICHARD: I think when the mother is eating, the baby eats. The food comes down in the belly.

MAURICE: Yeah, but Richard! And how would it be there in the first place? Though the person would eat.

T: Maurice, Maurice, I want you to stop now. There are other people who want to speak.

GERMAINE: I think. I think, that when the mother drinks, like Charles, the juice or milk. After she swallows, the baby gets it. And then I think the baby grows when she, like, drinks milk or something.

MAURICE: No. Then the mom would starve if all the food she digests goes into the baby.

GERMAINE: I don't think so.

CHARLES: The milk

ELI: Well, uh, the mother wouldn't starve because the baby, once it's inside her, it's kind of attached to her. 'Cause there are, like, tubes everywhere that are attached to her inside.

[MAURICE: No.]

ELI: Inside, and then, like all the food that's the leftover digested, goes into the baby. So, let's say the mother eats some lettuce, then all the leftover of the lettuce from digestion, goes into the, so the baby can have some food also.

MAURICE: I want to go back to where Richard said, to where Richard said his thing. What did you say? I forgot what you said.

RICHARD: What?

T: Well, then you should wait. Adam, do you want to get in there? Go right ahead.

ADAM: Uh, when it goes in, maybe she might feel the baby, like, sitting down, and it might give her an idea that it's eating, and she might eat some more so, so, she doesn't starve.

[CHARLES: Well, the mother will not starve, because the baby just eats it, and she, there's gonna be leftovers 'cause they can't eat a lot when they're really little. They can't, like, they can't eat like a ton of lettuce that their mom digests. They just eat a little, so the mom won't starve inside. They can only eat a little of it when they're that little, because they're like (showing size with his fingers), that big.]

[MAURICE: This is how big when they start, and they start digesting more food, and developing the shape of their body.]

T: Cindy, go ahead. (Cindy is an intern.)

T2: I'm having a really difficult time because there are three or four people talking at once so I can't follow anyone's conversation. Listen to each other!

ELI: Well, I agree with Charles. I mean, a baby, when it's not even out can't eat like one bite. It can only eat like, maybe, like one quarter of a bite.

MIKE: Like, the baby when it's inside of your body is only about that big. When it's first made, it just eats and eats and eats, and, and

(There are a lot of boys talking over each other, making the tape inaudible.)

T: Let's go back to the question. The question is: How does a baby grow inside the mother? And who has not had a chance? How does a baby grow inside? You've heard a few ideas.

DIANE: I sort of agree with Mia, that, that, but I have something to add to that. That the baby also can breathe inside her because there's air inside her, that she's breathing in and, before she lets it out, the baby gets it.

CHARLES: Yeah, the new air that she sucks in goes to the baby. Each second like you breathe, the old air comes out and the new air comes in. If you have a baby inside of you, the new air goes in.

T: Rachel wants to get in.

RACHEL: I think how the baby breathes is through the oxygen cord.

T: The oxygen cord, that cord?

RACHEL: Yeah.

MAURICE: The baby wouldn't, really wouldn't be able to breathe when it wasn't formed yet! It would be like, that big. It wouldn't have any place to breathe. It would at least need to get this big and have part of its shape.

MIKE: I agree that it has little tubes coming off of it that attaches to the mother that all the food and the oxygen go in. So what I think when it goes in, instead of just going in down to the lungs, it goes all the way to the baby, too.

ELI: Maurice, the baby doesn't have to breathe all the time. Because the baby doesn't breathe when it's an egg. It's not always breathing.

GERMAINE: Maurice, Maurice, Maurice, Maurice. I think how long the baby
   stays in the mother is how long it grows.
[MIKE: Yeah, it has to be that, 'cause like the more it grows. 'Cause you know
   how little babies are so small in the mother. Their hands are so tiny, their
   bones are so small. Sometimes they don't survive.]
[CHARLES: Mike, their hands on a ruler, they're about that big. That's how big
   their fingers are when they're first, when they're a li-, their fingers are
   that big.]
GERMAINE: It's just like caterpillars
(Several boys are talking at once.)
T: Go ahead.
GERMAINE: Just like caterpillars when they grow. They turn into a butterfly.
   You know how butterflies grow? It makes more sense if the baby grows
   like a butterfly.
T: Can you talk a little bit more about that? Can you say a little more about
   that? Can anyone help Germaine with that one?
MIKE: I think what he's trying to say is like,
GERMAINE: You know how caterpillars grow, and they turn into, like, big cat-
   erpillars?
ELI: I don't get it.
T: Ask him a question. That way he can say more.
ELI: We don't turn into humans and fly you know.
T: How do you mean?
ELI: Well, maybe we fly airplanes, but besides that . . . (Eli shrugs and smiles
   broadly at the group, his arms extended out from his side.)
MAURICE: Yeah, I sort of agree with Eli.
CHARLES: I do, too.
T: But I'm trying to understand what Germaine is saying because I think he's
   making a point by talking about caterpillars growing. What I want to
   know is, what's the one thing you want to say to us. You're not saying
   we're like caterpillars?
   (Germaine nods his head, signaling the negative.)
   No. You're saying something else. About how they grow and change. The
   point that I wanted to ask is kind of like that. In the body, in the mother's
   body, the baby doesn't start out looking like a baby, right? How does that
   baby grow and change shape and stuff inside? How does that happen?
DAN: The first day gets past and they get older and older, and then, when
   their birthday comes, they get bigger and bigger. When it's their birthday
   they get older.
CHARLES: It's sort of that way, I think. But they might, like, each time get bigger, like each birthday they might, like, if they're that big, they might get,
   like, that big, and then, like get more.
ELI: Maybe, maybe, now we're more talking like it might make sense. Take a
   bird. First it's an egg. Then it gets more. Then it gets its feathers, more
   hair, and gets bigger. Then it gets to be a grown-up bird. And then we
   get to be older. . . . We don't get to start all over. We just grow our hair
   and get bigger.

MIKE: Well, I kind of agree. In the end, first it's a yolk, and then it kind of, and then, like, then like, it gets like, little kind of, little bit of blood, and then the yolk kind of gets a shape, and then it turns into a bird and then it cracks open like a chicken egg. And then, like, and then, like, if maybe, maybe, if then, like when it gets cracked out, like our cockatiels when they're little they don't really look like the big ones. They don't have their things on their heads, or they hardly have any feathers. They look really ugly! And, but then, when they grow up, they get more feathers and everything.

ELI: Well, because the more it eats, and then it also gets fatter and changes, and he also gets bigger, and then maybe, hair will get longer.

T: Do you think it's eating then? Is it always eating?

References

Bakhtin, M. (1981). *The dialogic imagination*. Austin: University of Texas.

Barnes, D. (1976). *From communication to curriculum*. New York: Penguin.

Beveridge, W. I. B. (1950). *The art of scientific investigation*. New York: Norton.

Bragg, L. (1968). In J. Watson, *The double helix* (p. viii). New York: Atheneum.

Bruner, J. (1986). *Actual minds, possible worlds*. Cambridge, MA: Harvard University Press.

Carey, S. (1985). *Conceptual change in childhood*. Cambridge, MA: MIT Press.

Carey, S. (1986, October). Cognitive science and science education. *American Psychologist, 41,* 1123–1130.

Cazden, C. B. (1988). *Classroom discourse*. Portsmouth, NH: Heinemann.

Cazden, C., John, V., & Hymes, D. (Eds.). (1972). *Functions of language in the classroom*. New York: Teachers College Press.

Cobb, E. (1994). *The ecology of imagination in early childhood*. Austin, TX: Spring.

DeBoer, G. (1991). *A history of ideas in science education: Implications for practice*. New York: Teachers College Press.

Duschl, R. (1990). *Restructuring science education: The importance of theories and their development*. New York: Teachers College Press.

Edelglass, S., Maier, G., Gebert, H., & Davy, J. (1992). *Matter and mind: Imaginative participation in science*. Hudson, NY: Lindisfarne.

Edwards, D., & Mercer, N. (1987). *Common knowledge: The development of understanding in the classroom*. London: Methuen.

Fox-Keller, E. (1983). *A feeling for the organism: The life and work of Barbara McClintock*. New York: W. H. Freeman.

Gallas, K. (1994). *The languages of learning: How children talk, write, dance, draw, and sing their understanding of the world*. New York: Teachers College Press.

Gee, J. (1990). *Social linguistics and literacies: Ideology in discourses*. London: Falmer.

Gould, S. J. (1989). *Wonderful life: The Burgess Shale and the nature of history*. New York: W. W. Norton.

Hanson, N. R. (1965). *Patterns of discovery*. London: Cambridge University Press.

Holton, G. (1973). *Thematic origins of scientific thought: Kepler to Einstein*. Cambridge, MA: Harvard University Press.

Holton, G. (1978). *The scientific imagination: Case studies*. New York: Cambridge University Press.

Hymes, D., & Cazden, C. B. (1980). Narrative thinking and storytelling rights: A folklorist's clue to a critique of education. In D. Hymes (Ed.), *Language in education: Ethnolinguistic essays* (pp. 126–138). Washington, DC: Center for Applied Linguistics.

Kuhn, T. S. (1970). *The structure of scientific revolutions.* Chicago: University of Chicago Press.

Latour, B. (1987). *Science in action.* Cambridge, MA: Harvard University Press.

Latour, B., & Woolgar, S. (1979). *Laboratory life: The social construction of scientific facts.* Beverly Hills, CA: Sage.

Lemke, J. (1990). *Talking science: Language, learning and values.* New York: Ablex.

Linn, A. (1993, January 2). Interview on "All Things Considered."

Lynch, M. (1985). *Art and artifact in laboratory science: A study of shop work and shop talk in a research laboratory.* London: Routledge and Kegan Paul.

Mead, M. (1959). Closing the gap between the scientists and the others. *Daedalus, 88*(1), 139–146.

Medawar, P. (1982). *Pluto's Republic.* Oxford: Oxford University Press.

Morson, G. S., & Emerson, C. (1990). *Mikhail Bakhtin: Creation of a prosaics.* Stanford, CA: Stanford University Press.

Ochs, E., & Taylor, C. (1992). Science at dinner. In C. Kramsch & S. McConnell-Genet (Eds.), *Text and contexts: Cross-disciplinary perspectives on language study* (pp. 29–45). Lexington, MA: Heath.

Posner, G., Strike, K., Hewson, P., & Gertzog, W. (1982). Accommodation of a science conception: Toward a theory of conceptual change. *Science Education, 66,* 211–227.

Rothenberg, A. (1979). *The emerging goddess: The creative process in art, science, and other fields.* Chicago: University of Chicago Press.

Storey, R. D., & Carter, J. (1992, December). Why the scientific method? *The Science Teacher, 59*(9), 18–21.

Toulmin, S. (1972). *Human understanding.* Princeton, NJ: Princeton University Press.

Watson, J. (1968). *The double helix.* New York: Atheneum.

Wells, G. (1986). *The meaning makers.* Portsmouth, NH: Heinemann.

Index

Analogy, 46

Bakhtin, Mikhail, xi, 2, 3, 99
Barnes, D., 10, 11, 32
Beveridge, W. I. B., 13
Body language, 20, 23, 24
Bragg, L., 12
Brainstorming sessions, 21
Bruner, J., 10

Carey, S., 57, 80
Carter, J., 8
Cazden, C. B., 10
Child-centered approach, different levels of, 10–11
Coaches, teachers as, 82–96
Cobb, E., 14, 15, 43
Co-construction, of knowledge, 9, 11–12, 18, 29–31, 99
Collaboration, in co-construction, 9, 11–12, 18, 29–31, 99
Community
of learners, 3
theory and, 43–44
Curriculum
emergence of, 101
informal, building, 70–76

Davy, J., 15
DeBoer, G., 7
Discourse. *See also* Science Talks
acquisition of, 3
co-construction of, 9, 11–12, 18, 29–31, 99
reasons for, 9–12

scientific, 7, 12–16
Discussion. *See* Science Talks
Duschl, R., 8, 15, 42, 47

Early childhood experiences, 14–15
Edelglass, S., 15
Edwards, D., 11, 82
Einstein, Albert, 13, 14
Emerson, C., 3
Epistemology, 27–29, 45
"Expert" students, 23–25

Facilitators, teachers as, 18–19, 22–23, 82–96
Fox-Keller, E., 13, 14, 15

Gallas, K., 11, 12, 14, 43, 46, 101
Gebert, H., 15
Gee, J., 10
Gertzog, W., 44
Gould, S. J., 43

Hanson, N. R., 12, 13, 14
Heteroglossia (Bakhtin), 3
Hewson, P., 44
Holton, G., 13, 14, 15, 27, 41, 42, 43, 44
Hymes, D., 10

Imagination, in science, 14, 67–68
Intuition, in science, 14

John, V., 10

Knowledge
children's, viewing, 26–29

co-construction of, 9, 11–12, 18, 29–31, 99
prior, 52–54
theory versus, 55–56
Kuhn, T. S., 13

Language
research on, 10–11
of science, 8
Latour, B., 12, 13, 14, 42
Lemke, J., 8, 25, 42
Linn, Al, 41
Listening, 23
Literacy, research on, 10–11
Lynch, M., 13, 14, 43

Maier, G., 15
McClintock, Barbara, 13, 14
Mead, M., 9
Medawar, P., 7, 8, 12, 13, 41, 43
Mercer, N., 11, 82
Metaphor, 46, 65, 76–79, 86, 102
Metaphysics, of science, 15, 46
Morson, G. S., 3

Nonverbal responses, 20, 23, 24

Ochs, E., 43

Philosophy, of science, 15, 46
Posner, G., 44
Power relationships, 82, 92–94, 100

About the Author

Karen Gallas is a first and second grade teacher in Brookline, Massachusetts, and is also a member of the Brookline Teacher Research Seminar. She has taught children in the public schools of Massachusetts since 1972, with the exception of 4 years when she was a member of the faculty of the University of Maine. She received her doctorate in education from Boston University in 1981. Her work as a teacher researcher has focused on the role of the arts in teaching and learning, on children's language in the classroom, and on the process of teacher research. Her first book, *The Languages of Learning: How Children Talk, Write, Dance, Draw, and Sing Their Understanding of the World,* also by Teachers College Press, was published in 1994.